ALSO BY DEBORAH LEVY

THE POSITION
OF SPOONS

THE POSITION
OF SPOONS

And Other Intimacies

DEBORAH LEVY

FARRAR, STRAUS AND GIROUX
NEW YORK

Farrar, Straus and Giroux
120 Broadway, New York 10271

Grateful acknowledgment is made for permission to
reprint the following material:
Lines from *Paris: A Poem* (1920) by Hope Mirrlees, reproduced
by permission of Faber & Faber Ltd.
Lines from "The Couriers" from *Ariel* (1965) by Sylvia Plath,
reproduced by permission of Faber & Faber Ltd

Photograph on page 3: Colette © Tuul and Bruno Morandi /
Alamy Stock Photo.

Spoon art by MaKars / Shutterstock.com.

Library of Congress Cataloging-in-Publication Data
Names: Levy, Deborah, author.
Title: The position of spoons : and other intimacies / Deborah Levy.
Description: First American edition. | New York : Farrar, Straus and
   Giroux, 2024.
Identifiers: LCCN 2024008336 | ISBN 9780374614973 (hardcover)
Subjects: LCSH: Levy, Deborah. | Authors, English—20th century—
   Biography. | Authors, English—21st century—Biography. | LCGFT:
   Autobiographies.
Classification: LCC PR6062.E9255 Z46 2024 | DDC 823/.914 [B]—
   dc23/eng/20240511
LC record available at https://lccn.loc.gov/2024008336

Designed by Gretchen Achilles

Our books may be purchased in bulk for promotional,
educational, or business use. Please contact your local bookseller
or the Macmillan Corporate and Premium Sales Department at
1-800-221-7945, extension 5442, or by email at
MacmillanSpecialMarkets@macmillan.com.

www.fsgbooks.com
Follow us on social media at @fsgbooks

1   3   5   7   9   10   8   6   4   2

THE POSITION
OF SPOONS

BATHED IN AN ARC OF FRENCH LIGHT

COLETTE

I fell in love with her before I read any of her books.

To my teenage eyes smeared in the black kohl I believed made me look nihilistic and wasted (it was the era of punk after all and we were all in mourning for the future), Colette had a self-possessed kind of beauty that I felt she owned and hired to the photographer.

Even better as far as I was concerned, living as I did in the suburbs of London where everyone looked the same and even called their dogs the same name (there were three dogs called Spot in my street alone), Colette was a writer who looked like a movie star.

I looked nothing like her. Her dog was called Toby-Chien.

I don't know how I chanced upon this photograph. I do know it was a freezing December in 1973 and the central heating had broken down in our family house.

The doorbell rang and my mother shouted at me to let in the man who had arrived to fix the heating. He poked around in the cupboard where the boiler was and said, 'I officially condemn this boiler. The law says you've got to buy a new one.' Then he winked at me and switched it on. The pipes in the house started to whirr and clank like an old tractor. When I at last returned to my bedroom, I had to fight my way through the black smoke coiling out of my radiator.

Despite it being a very posed image, there was something about the way Colette had contrived its artifice that connected with me. She was a working writer who had a purpose in life. I could see immediately that she was enjoying the theatre of inventing herself to portray this purpose. This was of particular interest in that phase of my own life.

I was born in South Africa and grew up in Britain. When I glimpsed this photo at thirteen years old, I had lived in Britain for four years, not quite long enough to feel that I was English. Colette was presenting herself in a way that appealed to my teenage idea of what a European female writer might be like. Glamorous, serious, intellectual, playful – with a mean, sleek cat sitting on her writing desk amongst the flowers, all of them bathed in a glowing arc of French light.

When I started to read her books, all that was transgressive and sensuous in her writing blew like a wind from Burgundy, Paris and the South of France into the damp suburban gardens of London. Her affairs with women and her three marriages (the first to a perverse and corrupt bon viveur who signed her early novels as his own) meant she had one foot in and one foot out of the bourgeois life of her era. She became arthritic in middle age and often wore mannish open sandals with her elegant dresses, much to the agony of her more conventional second husband.

I knew none of this when I first glimpsed the photograph, yet somehow I intuited she'd had an experimental life.

What is the point of having any other sort of life, I thought to myself. Outside I could hear one of the dogs called Spot barking at a cat called Snowy. Twenty years later, when I read *The Vagabond*, I had cause to agree with her light but slyly deep assertion, 'I want nothing from love, in short, but love.'

Yes, what else is it we would want from love, apart from love?

Too many things, as it happens.

MARGUERITE DURAS

The purpose of language for Duras is to nail a catastrophe to the page.

She thinks as deeply as it is possible to think without dying of pain. It is all or nothing for Duras. She puts everything into language. The more she puts in, the fewer words she uses. Words can be nothing. Nothing. Nothing. Nothing.

It is what we do not do with language that gives it value, makes it necessary. Dull and dulling language is successful. Every writer knows this, makes a choice about what to do with that knowledge.

It's hard, sometimes even absurd, to know things, even harder to feel things – that's what Duras is always telling us. Her films are novelistic – voice-over, interior monologue – her fiction is cinematic: she understands that an image is not a 'setting' and that 'it has to hold everything the reader needs to know.' Duras is never begging with words but she is working very hard and calmly for us. Her trick is to make it all seem effortless.

Translated European literature was once shockingly hard to find in Britain. I was twenty-nine when I first read Marguerite Duras's 1984 masterpiece, *The Lover*, translated from the French by Barbara Bray. A revelation and a confrontation in equal measure, it was as if I had burst out of an oak-panelled nineteenth-century gentleman's club into something exhilarating, sexy, melancholy, truthful, modern and female.

If its cool, spare prose and flawless narrative design were somehow representative of the *nouveau roman*, largely associated with Alain Robbe-Grillet, it was clear to me that its major difference was that Duras did not distrust emotion. To write *The Lover* she drew on her early years living in Saigon with her impoverished mother and belligerent brothers. Structured as a kind of memoir, it is about a teenage girl living a peculiar colonial existence in French Indochina in the 1930s with her genteel but 'beggar family'.

She decides to make something happen and starts to wear a man's fedora hat and gold lamé shoes. In so doing, she suddenly sees herself 'as another'. It's a magic trick to separate from her deadening mother, and it works.

An elegant, wealthy Chinese man, twelve years her senior, is watching her on the ferry bus that crosses the Mekong River. When he risks offering her a cigarette, she notices that his hand is unsteady. 'There's the difference of race, he's not white, he has to get the better of it, that's why he's trembling.'

She wants to make him 'less afraid' so that he can do to her 'what he usually does with women' and, perhaps in return, he might sometimes buy her brothers and mother a meal? In one of the most devastating and brutally truthful seductions ever written, the Chinese financier who, she discovers, owns all the working-class housing in the colony, drives her in his 'funereal' limousine to his apartment on the edge of the city.

She undresses him, notices she desires him, panics, tells him he must never love her. Then she cries – about her mother's poverty and because she often hates her. *The Lover* does not just portray a forbidden sexual encounter of mind-blowing passion and intensity; it is also an essay on memory, death, desire and how colonialism messes up everyone.

I'm not convinced a book as incandescent as *The Lover*, more existential than feminist, would be published today. Not in Britain, anyway. Questions would arise. Are the characters likeable (not exactly), is it experimental or mainstream (neither), is it a novel or a novella? Fortunately for Duras, it didn't matter to her readers. It sold a million copies in forty-three languages, won the Prix Goncourt and was made into a commercial film.

Marguerite Duras was a reckless thinker, an egomaniac, a bit preposterous really. I believe she had to be. When she walks her bold but 'puny' female subject in her gold lamé shoes into the arms of her Chinese millionaire, Duras never covertly apologizes for the moral or psychological way that she exists in the world.

MY BEAUTIFUL BROTHEL
CREEPERS

When I was seventeen and bought my first pair of brothel creepers from Shellys, a high-street shoe store in London, I gazed at their two inches of thick black crêpe sole and knew I would never wear them with socks. It has always been very clear to me that people who wear shoes without socks are destined to become my friends and lovers. These sockless people have a kind of abandon in their body. They walk with zip. At the same time they manage to look both nonchalant and excitable. To not wear socks is to be alert but not hearty. To not wear socks is to not pretend that love is for ever.

If it's any consolation, people who do wear socks are probably better adjusted than their sockless brothers and sisters. They face up to things and always carry an umbrella when it rains.

The sockless are godless. So are brothel creepers, also known as 'Teddy-boy shoes'. To walk down the street in my very first pair made me feel like I was wearing a tattoo that marked me out for a meaningful life. I have bought many versions of them since, but twenty years later that first pair still lie intact on the top shelf of my shoe rack. Like jazz musicians they have improved with age. Not quite winkle-pickers, their leopard-skin tongue (V-shaped) is still seductive, ready to pounce and growl. To slip my naked foot into these shoes was to literally walk on air. My brothel creepers were beauty and truth, genius personified, never mind they were rock and bop, that was not the point, they were the metropolis, a ticket out of suburbia.

My brothel creepers made me feel sexy, serious, frivolous, confident. I wore them with tight black clinging dresses and I wore them with jeans. I wore them with pencil skirts and pinstriped trousers and I wore them to take out the garbage.

There is something in the brothel-creeper design that seemed to put the world in perspective. Their pointy black toes tapped to the beat of rebellion; the shoes my mother would never have worn, the shoes my father would never have worn, in fact the shoes not many girls wore but the ones who did were gorgeous. My narcissism was confirmed when, one afternoon, faint with hunger, I found myself waiting on the platform of a station somewhere in the sleepy shires. When I heard the train was going to be eleven minutes late, I ran over the bridge (in my beloved brothel creepers) to find something to eat at the local supermarket.

Everyone was old and if they weren't old, they looked like

they were. Except for the checkout girl in her checked overalls staring dreamily into the white strobes on the ceiling. Three minutes to go and her till roll runs out. As she stands up to get another one, I see she is wearing brothel creepers, too. Except hers are electric-blue suede and have even more attitude than my own. As I run for my train, I know she will get out of that village. Her shoes are a sign that she is making plans for a life elsewhere.

WALKING OUT OF
THE FRAME

She is an art student and she has booked a studio for a number of hours. She will have studied the floor and walls and the corners of walls and where the windows are positioned and how she is going to make the light work. She has a few plans (slow shutter speed, long exposures) but she's just going to play around. She is her own subject but she is embodying many other subjects and one of them is representation. Representation of the female form. This image is not a self-portrait of Francesca Woodman. She is using her body to figure things out.

Look at her. There she is. She is all there. She is all there but she's always trying to make herself disappear – to become vapour, a spectre, a smudge, a blur, a subject that is erased yet recognizable. She knows we know she's there and by constructing techniques to make herself disappear she knows she makes herself bigger. She makes herself bigger because we are searching for her. The artist, Francesca Woodman, has given us something to find. It's a dance, a theory, perhaps a Lacanian theory (*la femme n'existe pas*), a fiction, a provocation, an experiment, a joke, a serious question. Francesca Woodman, like all girls and women, wants to escape the frame.

She knows that when we look at this image we will want to find 'her' but the her we find is the art – the whole kinetic composition. I know she is art-directing everything, working out how to do her trick. She is alert, supple, aligned, poised. She has more or less seen this image before she has made it, or she has seen it in the act of making it, and she has probably felt this image for ever. All she has to do is find techniques to make it happen. If she's making herself present by making herself absent, it is easier to figure out that equation with maths or physics, but she's doing it with art.

The boots are there to land this ethereal image. It is so important to have a grip when we walk out of the frame of femininity into something vaguer, something more blurred. Francesca Woodman, the artist, can move freely in those boots but they also pull her down. The image would suffer without their presence. Actually, I am wearing boots that are quite similar as I write this. In about five minutes from now, I'm going to switch off my computer, lock the door of my writing shed and walk to the Tube station.

BELIEVE IT

Lee Miller was born in Poughkeepsie, New York, seven years after Freud published *The Interpretation of Dreams*. There is always something dream-like and inscrutable in photographs of her when she was young. She both hides from and gives herself to the camera. I want to keep on looking at Lee Miller because I'm not sure what I am looking at – her beauty, her poise, her hat, her melancholy gaze.

What was she going to do with all that beauty and talent? She became a fashion model to the distinguished photographers of her day in New York and then went off to study art in Europe. In Paris she worked with Man Ray, became his student, lover and model, collaborating on many extraordinary images that she probably is not credited for. She was publicly very modest about her own work, but perhaps she didn't feel that way inside.

After she left Man Ray, she established her own studio and hung out with the girlfriends of the surrealist male artists of her generation. It is Lee's photographs of Nusch Éluard and Ady Fidelin that rescue them from their roles as muses and mannequins. I always like coming across them when I look at the surrealist archives. And then there is the shock of some information to be found in Lee Miller's own biography. I don't want to believe it. There is a photograph of Lee as a child, wearing dungarees around the age of seven or eight, not long after she was raped by a 'family friend'. She stares at the camera, looking fragile and numb.

In 1944 she became a war correspondent with the US army, following the US infantry across a traumatized Europe. She was a witness. She pointed her camera at terrible things, at human history in the present tense.

As one of the few female combat journalists at the time, it was Lee Miller who photographed the liberation of Dachau and Buchenwald. She climbed up on to a truck and stood amongst the bodies to photograph the emaciated, dead prisoners.

The photographs were published in American *Vogue*, with the heading 'Believe It'.

VALUES AND STANDARDS

I began to wonder why a particular middle-aged woman of my acquaintance had eyes that seemed to want to disappear into her head. When her tiny peepholes tried to wriggle away from my gaze, I did not blame them for trying to hide, but it was odd talking to someone with shrinking eyes.

It became clear to me that she was in some sort of distress. I did not know her very well, but we sometimes met at the school gates when we picked up our young children. She was hyper-middle class, huge house, books on the shelves, art on the walls. It was as if she had told herself she did not suffer fools gladly (me) and that she stood for certain kinds of values and standards. She was not really very likeable. I began to think about how she had removed her eyes in the name of whatever it was she stood for.

It was possible that she did not want to look out of her

eyes and see the circumstances in her life that were unpleasant to her. I had witnessed the ways in which her husband could not be separated from the pleasure he took in undermining and humiliating her. It was as if he had told himself he did not suffer fools gladly (her) and that he stood for certain kinds of values and standards. If she had performed a complicated psychic operation in which she had removed her own eyes and saw the world and herself through his eyes, I wondered if there were times she put her own eyes back in again?

I began to think about my own eyes. There were times when they definitely became smaller. When my eyes became peepholes it was usually because other things had become bigger. Perhaps overwhelming. There is the phrase *to narrow the eyes*. It usually refers to taking the measure of something or someone, to see things as they actually are – to express doubt, disdain, perhaps to uncover a lie. Does this mean that we narrow our eyes in order to see things clearly? In which case, the Red Riding Hood story would go something like this:

What big eyes you have.
All the better not to see you.

What does this tell us about wide-eyed realists? Are they wide-eyed because they secretly yearn to see less, not more, despite having a great deal invested in the truth of their vision?

It is possible that the woman of my acquaintance who stood for certain kinds of values and standards did not want to know that the standards and values she had bought into might just slaughter her. Her eyes, which she had plucked out like Oedipus, were staring at her anyway.

KINGDOM COME

'Consumerism rules, but people are bored. They're out on the edge, waiting for something big and strange to come along . . . They want to be frightened. They want to know fear. And maybe they want to go a little mad.'

—J. G. BALLARD, *KINGDOM COME* (2006)

J. G. Ballard, England's greatest literary futurist, changed the coordinates of reality in British fiction and took his faithful readers on a wild, intellectual ride. He never restored moral order to the proceedings in his fiction because he did not believe we really wanted it. Whatever it was that Ballard next imagined for us, however unfamiliar, we knew we were in safe hands because he understood 'the need to construct a dramatically coherent narrative space'.

When I was a young writer in the 1980s, Ballard first came to my attention after I read his luminous, erotic story collection, *The Day of Forever*. It was so formally inventive that I would not have guessed it had been published in 1967. Nor did I know that the baffled conservative literary establishment of his generation had tried to see off his early work as science fiction. Ballard always insisted he was more interested in inner space than outer space.

When it came to anything by Ballard, genre really did not matter to me; his fiction could have been filed under 'Tales of Alien Abduction' or 'Marsh Plants' and I would have hunted it down. Despite our difference in generation, gender and literary purpose, it was clear to me that he and I were both working with some of the same aesthetic influences: film, surrealist art and poetry, Freud's avant-garde theories of the unconscious. I was just starting to write but Ballard made me feel less lonely. Perhaps more significantly we shared the dislocation of not being born in Britain. Home was the imagination. I too was attracted to the paintings of de Chirico and Delvaux, with their dreamplaces – empty, melancholy cities, abandoned temples, broken statues, shadows, exaggerated perspectives. Ballard was going to make worlds we had not seen before in British fiction. When asked, after the success of *Empire of the Sun*, why it took him so long to write in a less disguised way about his childhood experience at the internment camp in Lunghua, his beautiful answer was that it took him 'twenty years to forget and twenty years to remember'. Of course, images from Shanghai and the war were laid for ever inside him. I have always thought that his books, with the exception of *Crash*, which seems to me an abstract attempt to grieve for his dead wife, were already written in that one room he shared with his parents between 1943 and 1945. The reach of his imagination was never going to fit with the realist literary mainstream but I was always encouraged by his insistence that he was an imaginative writer.

> I believe in the power of the imagination to remake the world, to release the truth within us, to hold back the night, to transcend death, to charm motorways, to ingratiate ourselves with birds, to enlist the confidences of madmen.

Good on you, Jim. There is a great deal of rather strained legend-making when it comes to Ballard, but it is the witty, deadpan, open-minded American journalist and pianist V. Vale, founder of the tremendous RE/Search Publications and champion of Ballard since 1973, who in my view tracked his thought drifts most sensitively in various interviews. I have never regarded Ballard as a kind of psychogeographer of postmodernity; his most enjoyable fiction is more Dada than Debord.

> I believe in the impossibility of existence, in the humour of mountains, in the absurdity of electromagnetism, in the farce of geometry, in the cruelty of arithmetic, in the murderous intent of logic.

His highly imagined landscapes and abandoned aircraft and stopped clocks and desert sand were located in his head – and anyway he preferred driving fast cars to walking. He once sent me a photograph of the Heathrow Hilton and told me it was his spiritual home. What was it that Ballard offered to me as a young female writer? It is more to do with what he did not offer. He preferred social theory to social realism. I was not going to run to Ballard's books to learn how to write a 'well-rounded' character, for God's sake. His characters are more like tannoys to broadcast his arguments and ideas. But I did love his gloomy, unbelievable male psychiatrists, cinematically lit, groomed, suave and perverse, sipping a stiff gin and tonic while they observe (and possibly medicate) everyone else freaking out around them. The well-mannered narrators in the later novels (*Cocaine Nights*, *Super-Cannes*, *Millennium People*, *Kingdom Come*) are mostly mild, middle-class, manly men. Their destiny is to become inflamed Nietzschean men, excited to finally understand that they too would like to punch their fists through the boredom of the empty, greedy, good life with its fragile veneer of civilization.

Yet I have always regarded Ballard as quite a paternal writer, steering us through the ruins of his dystopias via the mindset of his apparently rational avatars – always endearingly baffled to discover their own suppressed urges. I enjoyed his noirish female characters, too (many of them doctors), enigmatic instead of domestic, emotionally unavailable, sexually experimental, sometimes tanned and thuggish, as in *Cocaine Nights*, or vulnerable but corruptible as in *Kingdom Come* – but the great thing is that they do not want the male lead to marry them and are never about to roast a chicken.

> I believe in the beauty of all women, in the treachery
> of their imaginations, so close to my heart.

All these years later, I still marvel at the eerie poetry of Ballard's prose. It lingers like a strange perfume over his concise, matter-of-fact sentences, more heightened in the earlier novels and short stories, but the bottom notes (petrol, anguish, desire, nightmares) are still present in the first three lines of his final and most didactic novel, *Kingdom Come*:

> The suburbs dream of violence. Asleep in their drowsy villas, sheltered by benevolent shopping malls, they wait patiently for the nightmares that will wake them into a more passionate world . . .

Kingdom Come is an exuberant, crazed, maverick, twenty-first-century restaging of Freud's *Civilization and Its Discontents*. We have our usual Ballardian narrator, a decent chap, former advertising executive Richard Pearson, who, while driving down the slow lane of the M25, is surprised to find the indicator ticking as if it has a mind of its own. Pearson obeys his car's invitation to turn down a slip road, which 'I had somehow known was waiting for me.' Ballard believed our unconscious plans a number of assignments for us. The slip road leads to the small motorway town of Brookfields, near Heathrow. Pearson's father, a retired air pilot, has been killed by a deranged mental patient who opened fire, apparently at random, on the crowds shopping at the Metro-Centre, a massive mall in the centre of this town. Pearson suspects there is more to find out about his father's death and begins his investigations – with the oedipal help of the attractive female doctor who attended to his dying father, and who for some reason has sex with his son.

There are no spaceships hovering above the Metro-Centre, with its 'humid, microwave air', but the minds of the citizens who shop there have definitely been abducted by hyper-consumerism.

> At the sales counter, the human race's greatest confrontation with existence, there were no yesterdays, no history to be relived, only an intense transactional present.

The former advertising executive starts to uncover the drives of the savage consumers of Middle England who lug home refrigerators, toasters, televisions, beat up Asian shopkeepers and lavish affection on the three giant teddy bears sitting in the atrium of the Metro-Centre. Naturally, these Disneyesque toys are pierced with bullet holes.

Kingdom Come is a brutal fairy tale in which 'a more primitive world' is 'biding its time'. The blades of knives on display in the mall's hardware store menacingly form 'a silver forest in the darkness'. Ballard explores the pre-rational nationalism that replaces politics, the mass spectacle of St George's flags waved at the endless parades and sports matches. 'No Sieg Heils, but football anthems instead. The same hatreds, the same hunger for violence, but filtered through the chat-show studio and the hospitality suite.'

It seems that for Ballard, the labyrinthine Metro-Centre is

as enthralling as de Chirico's brooding Italian archways and piazzas.

Once again he will chase his obsessions and try to convince us that the modern personality most likely to survive late capitalism will be the elective psychopath.

If Freudian theory is waving to us through the St George's flags, Ballard makes sure its fingernails are bitten raw. As he has often stated, his literary aim was to find the hidden wiring in the fuse box of modernity. In the case of *Kingdom Come*, consumerism slips into 'soft' fascism. As a former advertising executive, Richard Pearson knows that 'all he is good at is warming the slippers of late capitalism' and the future is 'a cable TV programme going on for ever', a barcode, CCTV camera and a parking space. And what about dreams?

The Metro-Centre is dreaming you. It's dreaming all of us.

Kingdom Come does nothing less than perform keyhole surgery on late capitalism's heart of darkness.

TELEGRAM TO A PYLON
TRANSMITTING ELECTRICITY
OVER DISTANCES

It is in my mind to tell you that you stand like a dancer, like an ogre, like a shaman, like a child in a rage. You are certain of your gravity. You are holding your breath. Stars lay their dust on you. Foxes play by your feet. Light passes through you. What holds you together might come unstuck as things that hold us together sometimes do.

It is in my mind to tell you that my daughter is watching *High School Musical* on the TV in North London. Right now she is arranging her facial muscles and body posture and vowels and consonants to become someone who can sing her way out of conflicts with bullies in the school playground. It is in my mind to tell you that my daughter's eyes look like oil wells lit at night. This is the earth we share and talk about in strange ways.

I transmit these thoughts to you from the marshes and silent canals of Hackney, East London, to the curved bay of Cádiz, Spain, and on and under and it is in my mind to tell you that all thoughts can be bent like a spoon.

A MOUTHFUL OF GREY

To stand in the centre of Russell Square Gardens, London, WC1, in the November rain is to summon all your losses in life. It will remind you of every time you have been abandoned, felt desolate, been in the wrong place at the wrong time.

A civic garden square gentles the pace of the city that surrounds it, holding a thought before it scrambles. Its punctuation is a pause in the life of the city. A place where the beginnings of a latent nervous breakdown can express itself and God can be glimpsed inside the body of a London pigeon. As you stare at the block of rat-grey sky above the naked winter trees and listen to the roar of traffic that circles the square (for this is a square in a circle), you will experience the vertigo of standing still while passers-by are on the move. Here in the square, wooden benches have been positioned under the trees. In the November rain those benches appear forlorn, damp, stuck with dying autumn leaves. At the far end of the square is the Gardens Café, its white plastic chairs stacked in a puddle of rain. One remaining plastic table and a broken umbrella have not yet been put away, reminding the public of the true purpose of the gardens: a place to convivially eat and drink al fresco in a square of old trees, to flirt, to rest, to think, to enjoy the general ambience of History and Scholarship via the universities and British Museum nearby.

Inside the café, which is open despite the weather, the walls are painted a deep Mediterranean blue. There is something about this garden square that resembles a deserted beach resort in winter. Fellini's film *La Strada* comes to mind. The roar of the traffic can sound like the ocean and the café has all the melancholy of a seaside tea room selling sun hats out of season.

Fellini called his film 'a kind of Chernobyl of the psyche', and while it would be an over-dramatic comparison with Russell Square Gardens on a grey day of ceaseless rain, lone London seagulls scream in the sky. It is possible to listen to the cadence of the traffic as if it were waves and imagine you are about to deliver a heartbreaking revelation to the person you most love.

If you stroll out of the gardens, be sure to cross the road and at least see the interior of what used to be called the Russell Hotel (it will change its name many times) opposite the gardens, on the corner of Southampton Row. Founded in 1898 and once sold as 'nineteenth-century charm with twentieth-century facilities', the spine of the hotel is a grand circular staircase built from a ripple of burnt orange marble. Enjoy the way your twenty-first-century shoes will sink into the twentieth-century carpet as you stroll past the wooden panelling and crystal chandeliers towards the Brasserie, which at one point in its history was named after Virginia Woolf.

Virginia (1882–1941), long neck, hair up, smoked roll-ups, often mocked for living in her mind. If you are thinking of staying in certain hotels nearby, living in your mind is probably the best place to be. Virginia Woolf killed herself by placing stones in the pockets of her raincoat and jumping into a river. What would she think about being remembered as a hamburger served with coleslaw and fries?

It is possible the burger made from mad English cows will sing, 'My heart is like a singing bird' as you bring this mouthful of heritage Bloomsbury to your lips.

THE PSYCHOPATHOLOGY
OF EVERYDAY CAFÉ LIFE IN
FREUD'S VIENNA

Is there a single silver teaspoon that has not stirred up the memory of seduction and rage? Is there a Fräulein in the house without vague, disabling despair? Ah, the fresh and full aroma of hysteria under a constellation of coffee cups!

May the waiter (calm, contemptuous, organized) please bring to the table the shivering *Sachertorte* with its dark, oily cacao.

Observe Herr K. in his great coat lined with fur, gazing at Frau K.'s petticoats, white as frothing alpine milk. Is he still in love with his mother? Does he wish to murder his father, who regularly engaged in bestial coitus with the governess?

Today Frau K. likes her coffee the Turkish way. As she lifts the small cup to her lips, her right arm freezes in mid-air. Oh no! Is this the same arm that pulled a handsome Herr closer to her breast when they embraced on the big wheel at the fair in the park?

Near-death trance, vertigo and strudel under the new clean light of electricity!

Observe Frau O., who, revived by the libido of yeast in the Kaiser bread rolls, is in flirtation with the family doctor. This kindly gentleman administers vitamin injections to her sister on the last Tuesday of every month. Watch how he gallantly presses Frau O.'s fingers to his lips and then rises to play billiards in the next room. Tomorrow at noon, these white-haired industrialists will send their clever, unhappy daughters (parental conflicts, the laws of society, lecherous uncles) to the curer of souls at Berggasse 19. There, they will learn that desire must not always win the day, but it always does.

There will for ever be a snake in the cake box.

THEM AND US

We owe a great deal to the grandly expressive female hysterics of the late nineteenth and early twentieth centuries. Their apparently inexplicable symptoms (loss of voice, paralysis of limbs, anorexia, bulimia, chronic fatigue, fainting fits, indifference to life) were asking subversive questions about femininity: What does it mean to be a woman? What should a woman be? Who is her body supposed to please and what is it for? If she is required to cancel her own desires, what is she supposed to do with them? Hysteria is the language of the protesting body.

At the start of Freud's career in patriarchal Vienna, he was under the impression there was one sexuality and that it was male. Fortunately, he changed his mind, but he humbly confessed that after thirty years of professional practice, he still did not know what women wanted. Yet Freud was witness to the most modern of female questions and conflicts.

Unlike his mentor, the pioneering French neurologist Jean-Martin Charcot, nicknamed the Napoleon of Neuroses (his pet monkey roamed the wards at the Salpêtrière Hospital), Freud encouraged his patients to speak freely and without censorship. This was no small matter considering how callously women had been silenced by the societal restrictions of their day and not least by their families, many of whom were sexual predators. We must thank these women for telling their stories to Freud in his consulting room in Berggasse 19.

Anna O., Emmy von N., Dora and Jane Avril (a dancer at the Moulin Rouge who was painted by Toulouse-Lautrec) all struggled with myths about female character and destiny. In their attempts to find words for disabling despair, Freud tuned in to their most awkward and shaming memories or reminiscences. Psychoanalysis was born when he discovered that it was possible to interpret rather than medicate symptoms that had no biological or neurological cause. As Freud describes in his *Introductory Lectures on Psychoanalysis*, the task of a psychoanalytic treatment 'is to make conscious everything that is pathogenically unconscious'. He never promised that the Talking Cure would make us happy, but he believed it might make us less miserable. If words are so powerful that they can make us pregnant (as Anna O. believed), it is not surprising that psychoanalysis has always paid the closest attention to the structure of language. Freud wanted to find the truths that had been dodged.

The diagnosis of hysteria, which began with Hippocrates in the fifth century BC, has now been erased from the *Diagnos-*

tic and Statistical Manual of Mental Disorders (DSM). Yet we all know that trauma (from the Greek for 'wound') has not gone away, and neither have the girls and women who self-harm.

If the birth of psychoanalysis offered methods to investigate the unconscious mind, there is no doubt that personal and political conflicts, and above all rage and hopelessness, continue to speak through the body in our own century.

Hysteria is not about them, it is about all of us.

Hysteria is dead! Long live hysteria!

ANN QUIN

I recognize some of my own influences in Quin's writing. Her literary taste and aesthetic enthusiasms were European – Duras, Robbe-Grillet, Sarraute – and I'm guessing she must have read some of Freud and R. D. Laing.

I know how lonely she must have felt in Britain at the time she was writing. No wonder she scarpered as soon as her debut novel, *Berg* (1964), had earned her a ticket to travel to Europe and America. I know she understood she was on to something new and that she took herself seriously, in the right way; she had a serious sense of her literary purpose.

Quin had worked as a shorthand typist for a while, just like my own clever, book-loving mother. Both women were born in the 1930s, and again, like my mother, Quin (apparently) applied to enter university as a 'mature student'. It was hard for a working-class woman to get herself an education. Even Virginia Woolf found it a struggle to achieve a formal education, though her father had a well-stocked personal library. Presumably Quin made use of public libraries – and she would have read everything that John Calder, her heroic publisher, might have slipped her way.

Quin was reaching for something new and bewildering in each of her four published novels – the effort and exhilaration of that reach must have sustained her when life was tough. It is not vulgar to comprehend that she was ambitious for her work. Obviously, she put in the hours to design composition and cadence, to find a conceptual scheme to hold her ideas, to explore new possibilities for satire, shifts of viewpoint and voice. That's what writers are supposed to do.

It would be progress if we could stop the rhapsodizing of Ann Quin and just read her books without having to defend them. It's hard not to defend them, though. Few critics gave her books the respect of a close reading. It was as if Quin was culturally forbidden to actually possess a coherent literary purpose. The word 'experimental' kept her nicely in her place.

As it happens, I believe that if she had managed to swim back to the cold pebbles on Brighton beach that day she drowned, she would have gone on to write books that were nearer to herself. I want to know more about what it takes to want to swim home and I know Quin could have told me.

A TO Z OF THE DEATH DRIVE

A PERILOUS ROAD TRIP THROUGH DEATH, CELEBRITY AND THE AUTOMOBILE

A

Automobile, Anger, Accident, Acceleration

You are an accident waiting to happen. You are a complete wreck. What is driving you to do this? Will the automobile (a fusion of libido and machine) ever lose meaning as a sexualized instrument to be controlled and mastered? Or is it merely a transitional object such as a teddy bear, doll or soft blanket – the objects that helped us separate from our mothers? Our childhood dolls and toys survived being loved, loathed and mutilated – we gave them names, personalities, made up lives for them to live on our behalf. We pulled their arms and legs off, hacked off their nylon hair, turned their heads the wrong way round. And then we cuddled and kissed them and left them out in the rain. The automobile simply can't survive this kind of behaviour. The design of your anger is as important as the design of your car. Remember, I am only a Mercedes SLS AMG. I do not have advanced emotions and I do not want sex with you. If you crash me I will be unmasked as a totally inanimate thing and you will be unmasked as someone who thought your four-wheel-drive system loved you unconditionally.

> It was as if that great rush of anger had washed me clean, emptied me of hope, and gazing up at the dark sky spangled with its signs and stars, for the first time, the first, I laid my heart open to the benign indifference of the universe.
>
> —ALBERT CAMUS, *L'ÉTRANGER* (1942)

B
Marc Bolan, J. G. Ballard

Just as Marc's famous lyrics claimed, we too could ride a white swan and fly away from the parents who made us cry. Our tears were righteous, our thighs were thin. We were the children of the revolution and life was too short and brutal to take any notice of the posters forbidding 'petting' at the Victorian swimming pool down the road. Marc's voice was not really a voice, it was an attitude and it got us through double maths. When we painted our nails green it was for him. Bolan died on 16 September 1977 at 3.50 a.m. when his car hit a sycamore tree near Barnes Common, London. In ancient Egyptian religion the sycamore was regarded as a personification of the goddesses Nut, Isis and Hathor. Early paintings show them reaching out from a tree to offer the deceased food and water. The 'death tree' on Barnes Common was made into a roadside shrine by his fans.

Ballard's post-traumatic novel *Crash* (1973) was described by its author as the 'first pornographic novel based on technology'. The writer Ballard stages and repeats a number of violent car crashes that always end with his wounded and bloody drivers eroticized by their own death drives. Ballard probably agreed with Freud's notion that we all take pleasure in smashing things up. He knew the car was more than a car and went into head-on collision with Thanatos and Eros. Bourgeois English literature, with its liking for Victorian bonnets and keeping the unconscious in its place (under the bonnet), suggested the author needed to see a psychiatrist.

> Science and technology multiply around us. To an increasing extent they dictate the languages in which we speak and think. Either we use those languages, or we remain mute.
>
> —J. G. BALLARD, *CRASH*

C

Eddie Cochran, Albert Camus

Son of an Algerian cleaner, Albert Camus won the Nobel Prize for Literature. Camus was killed in a road accident in 1960 while travelling from Provence to Paris with the manuscript of his unfinished novel, *The First Man*, packed in his briefcase. His publisher was driving the car. Police noted the dashboard clock in the vehicle had stopped at 1.55 p.m. when it slipped off the wet road. Camus, who was now a tragic celebrity as well as a celebrity of political thought, was found to have an unused train ticket in his coat pocket. Whether we are inclined to make more meaning or indeed desire less meaning from the death sites of the famous, we still wish Camus had boarded that train.

Eddie Cochran ('C'mon Everybody') is sometimes described as 'James Dean with a guitar'. Eddie didn't even get to crash his own car. In 1960 he travelled to the UK to tour with Gene Vincent. Early one morning in Wiltshire, England, his taxi suffered a burst tyre, veered off the road and crashed into a lamp post. Eddie was twenty-one, and though he probably couldn't wait to get out of Wiltshire, we can be certain he didn't want this kind of exit.

D

James Dean

Kenneth Anger owned a mangled piece of Dean's cursed Porsche Spyder, bought for $300.

E

Ego

A passenger in any sort of car needs the driver to have a strong ego. Ego in this sense does not mean someone who is insufferably full of themselves. In Freud's structure of the psyche, the ego is the rational side of the mind which tries to come to terms with the fact that we can't always get what we want.

Mick Jagger knew this when he sang, 'No, you can't always get what you want' with Keith Richards in 1968. If you can't always get what you want, luscious lips are a blessing. Thin lips might make you look bitter and twisted. The ego on the road tries not to be bitter and twisted. It knows it has to compromise. It is in touch with the reality principle (red traffic lights mean stop) and tries to swat away the smoky voice of the id when it tells the ego to go faster and how about a swig of bourbon? The id is screaming, 'I want it, I want it!' but the ego is calmly explaining, 'You can't have it.' These are the conflicts your driver experiences on any sort of car journey. As a passenger, if you think the teenage id will win, better to get out fast and catch the Tube. It's not what you want, but it's what you need to do.

F
Fame, Fifteen Minutes, Fuel

Fifteen minutes is plenty of time to flirt with the fatal seduction of fame – needing your fans more than they need you is unsightly after a while. No matter how many trillions of gallons of fossil fuels are poured into fame, somehow its tank is never full.

G
God, Global Positioning Systems

God is a pair of (hidden) hands on the steering wheel, an ageless chauffeur driving us to an unknown destination. We will not know where the bathroom is when we arrive. God is free thought and God is a global positioning system inside us.

Those of us who believe in sat nav have to hope that when 'the voice' leads us away from the main road to a dirt track that leads to the edge of a high cliff, it knows what it's doing.

H

Haunt, Horoscopes, Highway

Fatal crashes haunt the highways of the world. Beeping police radios, twisted metal, exploded windows, the staring panicked eyes of the wounded. It doesn't bear thinking about, so we read horoscopes to know what lies on the road ahead. We want to hear the squeal of the tyres before they squeal.

I

Id

Like the ignition, the id is always turned on.

J

Jayne Mansfield

Jayne Mansfield died on 29 June 1967 when the driver of her Buick smashed into a trailer spraying the swamps of New Orleans with anti-mosquito insecticide at 2 a.m. During the late 1950s, the front bumpers of some American cars came with extensions that resembled a pair of large conical breasts. These were nicknamed 'Jayne Mansfields'. The Buick used to be displayed at various car shows with the bloodstains still splashed across the seats.

K
Grace Kelly

Alfred Hitchcock had a thing for what are sometimes called icy virginal blondes, and actress Grace Kelly was one of them. Kelly starred in Hitchcock's *Rear Window* and *Dial M for Murder*. Her career as an Oscar-winning actress would later be forbidden by her husband, Prince Rainier III of Monaco. When Kelly married her prince, Hitchcock declared himself 'very happy that (Princess) Grace has found herself such a good part'. Monaco is where Tintin might wear a beret on a secret assignation to find a diamond necklace hidden in a baguette. Kelly's catastrophic accident on the road between Monaco and Roc Agel in 1982 was apparently caused by failed brakes. In fact she had a stroke at the wheel of her ten-year-old Rover, which eventually tumbled a hundred feet down a ravine.

L
Liberty/Life

Greater liberty, greater fruitfulness of time and effort, brighter glimpses of the wide and beautiful world, more health and happiness – these are the lasting benefits of the motor-car.

—HERBERT LADD TOWLE,
'THE AUTOMOBILE AND ITS MISSION' (1913)

I want to live the rest of my life, however long or short, with as much sweetness as I can decently manage, loving all the people I love, and doing as much as I can of the work I still have to do. I am going to write fire until it comes out of my ears, my eyes, my noseholes – everywhere. Until it's every breath I breathe. I'm going to go out like a fucking meteor!

—AUDRE LORDE, *A BURST OF LIGHT: AND OTHER ESSAYS* (1988)

M
Mid-life Crisis

You've bought a motorbike, stopped shaving, asked your PA to order you some literature written by women. This is because your young girlfriend has pointed out that every book on your shelves is by a male author. You play St. Vincent on your media system (you prefer Van Morrison) and dream of a hearty boeuf bourguignon as you head off for a vegan curry with the new love of your mid-life. Her name is Nadia.

N

Nadia says she's poly and rides a bicycle.

O
Oral Sex

A super sport that should be included in the Olympic Games. Unlike throwing the javelin or jumping the high bar, everyone can do it. No one's house has ever been destroyed to build a stadium for this particular sport, because it can take place in an automobile.

P

Jackson Pollock

Jackson Pollock was battling with booze and depression when he remarked to a friend, 'I've gone dead inside, like one of your diesels on a cold morning.' Pollock was speeding wildly in his green Oldsmobile convertible coupe when it crashed along an East Hampton road in 1956, hurtling him fifty feet in the air. He smashed his skull on a white oak tree and was instantly killed. His girlfriend, Ruth Kligman, suffered a fractured pelvis but survived. Some newspaper reports at the time framed Pollock as a suicidal trickster. He could have done without this sort of thing. When Pollock laid out his massive canvases on the floor, it was into them that he poured his life and death.

Q

Questions

What are we to do with the uncivilized death wish that simmers within us even though we always say please and thank you? Freud did not believe that accidents were chance events. All accidents in his view are manifestations of the death drive, the urge to walk into traffic when we cross the road or stand too near the edge of the platform when waiting for a Tube. He even came to believe that to suffer from vertigo on a mountain is to suffer from the unconscious urge to throw ourselves off it. Ballard agrees. 'Deep assignments run through all our lives . . . there are no coincidences.'

R
Right-hand Side of the Road

About a quarter of the world drives on the left-hand side, mostly the old British colonies. It was believed by the ancients that evil spirits lived on the left side of man and the gods lived on the right side. For the Romans, left meant sinister and corrupt – which is probably what the colonized thought of the British.

S
Shrines

In every pile-up we confront our own anxieties and fleetingly review the meaning of our own lives. Roadside shrines to the deceased are assembled. Car-crash victims become saints. We want to know the details of the collision in order to piece the fragments together. In this sense a car crash often becomes a fiction that is of equal interest to lawyers, poets, forensic scientists and shop workers.

T
Trauma

To experience trauma is to have knowledge we do not want. When we repeat the details of a crash and say out loud what happened, we feel we have more control over this unwelcome knowledge. It is well known that if an aeroplane crashes, investigators search for the cockpit voice recorder, also known as the 'black box', to reveal details of the events preceding the accident. When we repeat our memories of a crash, either experienced or witnessed, we are the black box.

U
U-turn, Unconscious

Hansel and Gretel laid out a trail of bread in the forest so they could do a U-turn and find their way home. Birds ate the bread (road markings) and the wicked witch nearly ate Hansel and Gretel. The car is a womb to protect us from the wicked witch that lives in the forest with her green-eyed owls. Attempt to run the hag over and you will fall asleep at the wheel for a hundred years. Your dreams unfold at three mph. Deer slumber on the roof of your Volvo. Woodpeckers bury their beaks in the windscreen. Spiders spin webs in the wheels. If dreams are the royal road to the unconscious, it doesn't matter what kind of car you drive, you will always get there in the end.

V
Voyeur

To be a voyeur is to observe others without being seen ourselves. Sometimes it implies a clandestine sexual interest. A voyeur is 'one who looks' at an intimate action without any of the risks involved with engaging directly with intimacy. Yet to observe the fallout from a car crash does have its risks. It gives us voyeuristic spectators an intimate sense of our un-doing, a foreboding collision with the spectre of our own ending. As we gaze in horror at the shattered debris on the road, there is often a shameful glass shard of excitement and curiosity inside us too. It is as if the crash is the final edit of the imaginative games we all played as children (faking being dead, peek-a-boo) to prepare ourselves for the impossibility of accepting death.

W
Warhol, Wreck

In Warhol's silk-screen paintings of car crashes – *Green Disaster* (1963), *Orange Car Crash* (1963), *Saturday Disaster* (1964) – the artist appropriated news photographs of everyday anonymous car crashes, repeating the trauma in multiple prints – as if the act of seeing them over and over numbs us to the spectacle of tragedy and death.

X

A kiss under the bright night stars.

Y
Yawning

In the Middle Ages it was believed that the devil entered our mouths every time we yawned. A hand clapped over this hole

in our face was a kind of central locking device to stop mug-
gers getting in. In the post-Industrial Age we know that yawning is caused by lack of oxygen. Therefore, yawning in an
automobile suggests the windows should be hastily opened.
Yawning is also contagious. A passenger must never yawn too
near the driver.

Z
Sleep

In his essay *Le Mythe de Sisyphe* (1942), Camus wrote, 'We
value our lives and existence so greatly, but at the same time
we know we will eventually die, and ultimately our endeav-
ours are meaningless.' When we stare in morbid fascination
at photographs of car crashes, particularly those involving a
celebrity presence, what is it we are hoping to find? It is possible the missing person we are searching for in the pile-up is
ourselves.

MIGRATIONS TO ELSEWHERE
AND OTHER PAINS

Down in the tunnels of Woolwich in South-east London, Alice did not know how to speak to the white rabbit. She tried a few phrases in French, Italian and Spanish from her European Dictionary, but the white rabbit looked confused.

He started to not so much lick his paws, as eat them. This was all the more alarming because he had gloves on. The rabbit had stuck his left paw into his mouth and was making strange sounds in his throat. Alice had asked him in the German language to show her the way to the nearest bus station. The rabbit spat out his paw, gathered his little Chinese silk fan to his chest and began to run. Alice ran after him as fast as she could in her shiny black shoes, kicking up a haze of Woolwich dust behind her. When the rabbit ran in zigzags, she ran in zigzags. When he ran in circles, she ran in circles. The white rabbit seemed to know that this was a useless chase. He suddenly stopped and started to search for something in his waistcoat pocket.

'Where are you looking for?' Alice said in English.

'I'm off to my other life,' the rabbit finally stuttered in an irritated voice, all the while patting the pockets of his waistcoat.

'Really?' She watched curiously as he took out a cigarette from a pack called 'Extra' and lit up with his gloved paw. For a while Woolwich disappeared under the strange milky-blue smoke of the rabbit's Extra. She could just see the tips of his ears poking through. 'Where is your other life?'

'Elsewhere.'

Alice tossed back her long hair. 'What does Elsewhere look like?'

'I don't know too much about the landscape.' The rabbit waved his paw in a nonchalant manner.

'Oh. So you haven't been there yet?'

Alice was learning all about stamina in Woolwich. When the rabbit took off again, this time with an Extra dangling from his lips, she had taught herself how to jog by his side. She watched the breathless bobtail check his stopwatch and mutter, 'Always remember to pull time backwards or forwards as appropriate to the place of destination.'

'What is the time in Elsewhere?'

The rabbit ignored her, inhaling hard on his Extra, eyes firmly fixed on the ground. Alice wondered if he had been used in a science experiment and become addicted to cigarettes as a result. She noticed that his whiskers were trembling.

'Well, I can give you some phrases,' offered Alice, waving

her dictionary. And then she remembered. 'Except I don't know what language they speak in Elsewhere.'

'They speak the language of Elsewhere,' replied the lachrymose, red-eyed one.

As they promenaded through Woolwich, a can of lager on a table caught Alice's green eye. She passed it to the silent, brooding rabbit.

'Perhaps you should have some of this? It might loosen your tongue and you can tell me more about Elsewhere.'

'Don't mind if I do,' said the rabbit. Alice opened the can and passed it to him. He grasped the can with his gloved paws (during the walk he had squeezed one of his gloves off and then very slowly put it on again) and raised it to his thin little lips.

'My mind is growing bigger,' he whispered. 'I can feel it growing right now.'

'So talk to me,' Alice demanded, and just so she could keep up, took the tiniest swig too.

'No!' The rabbit became more assertive. 'I will not say another word until you tell me who you are.'

'Well, I'll have a go!' Alice put her hands on her hips so she would not be tempted to bite her nails while she spoke. 'I live in England but I was born in Africa. I am a girl. I live with my mother, who is divorced from my father. I do have a sister. She's saving my Friday chocolate for me and I'm going to eat it when I get home. And I have two brothers. One lives in Mexico, the other in High Barnet, which is on the Northern line. Actually, I don't really know very much about myself. I don't know what it is I want to know and whether what I do know is worth knowing.'

The white rabbit thought about this for a while. 'Are you African, English or European?'

To his surprise, the girl started to cry. There seemed to be no end to the tears inside her. They fell down her cheeks and wet her black, shiny shoes. 'May I kiss you?' The rabbit made the request in a matter-of-fact manner.

Alice was curious. She had never been kissed by a rabbit, but she was in Woolwich and there were no brochures to tell her what to expect.

'OK.'

The rabbit stubbed out his Extra and bared his teeth. 'I tried ringing the Stop Smoking programme,' he murmured in her ear. 'But I kept getting the wrong quit line. Italian on Monday, Gujarati Tuesday, German Weds, Polish Thurs, Swahili Sunday. And I sleep on Saturdays.'

As he pressed his moist, round nose against her long, dry nose, Alice knew she was in for a big surprise. Even though new technologies predicted the end of biology, or something like that, she suddenly felt the difference between her heartbeat and that of the little beast attempting to kiss her.

For a start his lips were very thin and narrow and her lips were thick and wide. It was OK if she shut her eyes but when she peeped them open she stared straight into his small pink eyes with their bone-white lashes. He was staring hard at her. Straight into her half-shut green eyes. As much as she tried to think otherwise, it was clear to her that they were very, very different.

And then there were his whiskers to contend with. They kept tickling her jaw and some of them actually got into her mouth and pierced her gums. The other strange sensation was his ears. They were pointing upwards, very alert, like someone who is shocked. 'That's enough kissing for the moment,' she said sternly.

White rabbit thought so too. He found Alice bald, covered as he was with fur. Another thing. Her ears were strangely spaced at the side of her head and were not very expressive. These were difficult things to talk about, so instead he took a swig from the can of lager, took out his fan and waved it snappily across his face. 'My mind is very big now,' he yelped. 'I have inner immensity.' Alice wiped her mouth on her sleeve. 'The world inside me is bigger than the world outside me,' the rabbit continued.

'Is that where Elsewhere is?' Alice thought she was on to something. 'Is Elsewhere between your ears?'

'Perhaps,' the white rabbit conceded.

'That's no good. How can you bring me back a souvenir then?'

The rabbit fanned his face in gloomy silence.

Alice heard herself sound like someone who wasn't her, but as she didn't know who she was anyway, she thought she'd just have to go with the flow of her new Knowing Tone – which was a useful disguise for not knowing anything at all. The rabbit stroked the lining of his waistcoat and hummed as she developed her tone.

'Is Elsewhere better than Woolwich then, rabbit?'

'Oh yes.'

'Why is it better?'

'Elsewhere is the life I have never lived. The life I most want.'

'You might as well eat your head.' Alice laughed. The rabbit gathered himself up. He looked taller than he appeared to Alice when she first glimpsed him running through Woolwich. He pointed at her challenging, staring eyes with his fan and found her quite hideous. There was something about the certainty with which she expressed her opinions that made him want to crack her neck tendons with his upper incisors. As it was the stranger Alice who had kindly introduced him to these unfamiliar feelings, he felt obliged to introduce her to his rapidly expanding mind.

'You should know that I have inner immensity because I have gathered all my passions and longings into myself and with them I have built Elsewhere.'

White rabbit seemed to expect a standing ovation, because he put his gloved paws to his lips and blew kisses to an imaginary crowd.

'Well,' declared Alice. 'Hmm. Do you think I could try one of your Extras?'

The rabbit took out his pack and counted the cigarettes. 'Yes, madam,' he replied flamboyantly, and then to Alice's astonishment tried to sell her five disposable cigarette lighters for the price of one. Taking a puff of the Extra, Alice found herself filled with strange sensations and thoughts she could not chase fast enough.

'The fact is, when you arrive in Elsewhere you will be a stranger. You will be "the rabbit from elsewhere".'

'I can see you are a very tense sort of girl,' the rabbit muttered while inhaling another Extra. 'As I have told you at some length – but not as long as my Extra, which offers a little bit more, that is the whole point of extra – Elsewhere is my way of experiencing life itself!'

Alice pointed at the rabbit's little paws. 'You should take off your gloves and get real.'

The rabbit blinked. 'Yes. That is the name of my house in Elsewhere. "Villa Real".'

White rabbit lay down and rested his head that contained his inner immensity against his folded gloved paws. He meant to explain to the girl that he carried his homeland with him at all times. Consequently, his head was very heavy, and he fell asleep before he could even floss his teeth.

When white rabbit awoke from what turned out to be a dreamless sleep, he was surprised to find himself feeling desolate. Even more surprising were the tears that hurried down his cheeks and wet his fur. He gulped for air and licked his smarting gums, which really did feel as if they were not going to hold his teeth for much longer. There was no doubt about it. He was going to have to change the lifestyle of his inner immensity.

He was also extremely nervous about his gums deporting his teeth. Apart from needing his teeth, he felt their right and proper place was in his mouth. He did not want to carry his molars in his waistcoat pocket, because that is not where teeth should be. He parted his lips and lifted his little paw to prod his tender gums. The pain made him wince. There was no doubt that his back teeth were mobile. He could wiggle them quite easily. They were loose. They were going to roam. This fact appalled him. After ten minutes had passed, he decided that the next ten minutes were not going to get any better so he might as well have an Extra.

He shuffled about, patting the earth of Woolwich with his gloved paw, looking for his box of cigarettes. The first three puffs put him right. His tears dried up. His breathing settled down. His spirits lifted. But when he got to the fourth puff, he began to realize that the misery that had visited him in his sleep had not departed. Every next puff on his Extra just put off the misery that lurked between puffs. His Extras were not enough. But how could he get hold of extra Extras? It was as if his trustworthy brand had shrunk to Xtra rather than Extra.

Another thing. The rabbit sat down and tried to build a little bit more of Elsewhere. This is what he usually did when he was feeling glum. The new ballroom he was adding to Villa Real felt flimsy, not as solid as it should be. If he were to push the walls of the new extension with his paw, it would fall over, and worst of all, fall over noiselessly.

Rabbit found himself moping now and the tears were returning, this time very potent tears. It was as if the fluid oozing from his tear ducts was concentrated with some kind of despair, and this despair was like a homeopathic remedy. Lick a little teardrop and he would consume a small, controlled portion of his own misery to combat the larger misery spreading through his whole being. He looked round for a container into which he could splash some of these unwelcome tears.

His pink right eye saw a little bottle on the table with the label 'Cry into me'. As he did this absurd action, placed his eye over the top of the bottle and then wept so the tears dripped through, rabbit knew his tears were a message. A message in a bottle. He was going to have to accept that he lived and breathed in Woolwich and make himself a permanent resident there. The plaque that infected his gums, eroding them slowly day by day, had spread to his mind. The white rabbit took off his white gloves. He rolled them into a ball and tucked them into each other.

But what about Elsewhere, the place he most yearned to be? It was gone and he had no map to find it again. To think that Elsewhere had been destroyed, not by the Elsewhere Liberation Army but by his own psychic uprising.

Meanwhile, Alice found herself struggling with every muscle of her girl body to get out of Woolwich. There were no doors with 'exit' written on them to guide her. Nor were there windows or stairs or escalators or lifts or adults in uniform to give her directions. She intuited that she was going to have to dirty her hands with the soil of Woolwich and start digging. Once she had made this decision, she felt calmer. She knelt on the earth and started to dig with her hands. The tunnels of Woolwich were not as solid as they looked. To her surprise the soil came away easily and she dug faster and faster until she had created a large hole, her long hair trailing in the earth. While she dug she thought about white rabbit and how he had actually run away from her. Pitter-patter on his little feet. She should have grabbed him by his ears and searched his waist-coat for the packets of Extras and five disposable cigarette lighters. It occurred to her the only thing to do now was to plunge her head right into the hole she had created and push and push until she saw a crack of blue sky, which would be a sure sign she had heaved herself home.

This was how white rabbit found her. All he could see were Alice's shins stuck upright like a strange shrub growing in the tunnels of Woolwich. He knew at once that she was stuck. What he had to do was give the girl a push. After all he didn't want her to hang around wanting conversations with him. Oh no, not at all. The rabbit stuck a paw on the back of each of Alice's knees and bending his own knees to help his little body take the strain, gave her a good push. The buttons sprang off his waistcoat but he didn't care. He was going to have to twist her to the right and left, like a corkscrew. In fact he pushed and twisted the small girl's shins with such force he broke a blood vessel in his eye. Down she went. There she goes. All of Alice slipping through, except for her patent-leather, shiny shoes. They had somehow come undone in her struggle to exit, the buckles loosening, the shiny shoes slipping off her heels and then her toes and tumbling to the ground.

Oh, what lovely silver buckles! Panting slightly from his recent physical exertion, white rabbit slipped his little feet into Alice's shoes and found they fitted perfectly. The bobtail licked his whiskers as he took a few jaunty steps in his new footwear. The little black straps looked smart fastened against his white fur ankles. He experimented with a few shuffling dance steps, fanning his naked paws in front of his chest. He even felt better about his wobbly teeth. If the worst happened and they deported themselves from his gums, at least his feet would distract attention from his slack rabbit lips. He stroked his dishevelled fur with a dampened paw and, holding his little bottle of tears against his chest, strode bravely into the centre of Woolwich.

A ROAMING ALPHABET FOR
THE INNER VOICE

A is for Apollinaire who insisted that desire is the authentic voice of the inner self.

A is for Actor.

The actor and the murderer have something in common. We want to look at them, but more, we want to look inside them.

B is for Blush.

To blush is to become another centigrade. Humiliation or any strong feeling is a change in the climate of the body. And so is desire.

———

C is for Chronology.

The plot to this story starts on the letter J. If you want to skip down the page, that's okay. If you can be bothered you will get more out of this if you read D, E, F and I first.

D is for Desire.

When it comes to desire we are all in a soap opera and the script is always the same. 'I don't want to hurt you but I will. I am sorry because you are a good person but I am not sorry enough.'

E is for Eczema.

Eczema is the nervous system written on the outside of the body.

F is for Forgery.

That's all of us.

I is for Imitation.

Those of us who cannot imitate, lack imagination. We cannot see outside our own manner – we are nasty little nationalists.

———

J is for John.

L is for Love.

On Tuesday evening at 7.50 p.m. John and I went to see the film *A.I. Artificial Intelligence* by Steven Spielberg and Stanley Kubrick. We sat next to each other in the dark, close but separate. The film was about a robot boy made in a laboratory who was special because he was programmed to be able to love. His adopted mother grew frightened of her robot son's affection and abandoned him in the woods. Years later the robot boy is discovered at the bottom of a frozen river by strange and beautiful creatures that are artificial life. They have tall, thin bodies, similar to the figures in early cave paintings, and they are very respectful to the boy robot. They realize he is their last contact with human beings because it was a human who programmed him. I don't know what happened next except that John was drinking a can of lager and I had shut my eyes. I had shut my eyes because I realized John and I were artificially and intelligently in love. We were the artificial intelligence who needed to find the robot boy because he was programmed to love. He had something inside him that we needed to be inside us.

M is for Melancholy.

I knew John and I needed to have a conversation.

———

M is for Marriage.

When aeroplanes crash the emergency team look for the black box, which holds a record of the pilot's last conversation. I imagined that the conversation John and I needed to have would be found in the black box that was flung to the bottom of a glacier from the crashed aeroplane of our marriage. It falls through space and time and is dug out of the ice by artificial life who gather round to listen to the sad, strong voices of human beings in pain.

M is for Mystery.

It doesn't take an alien to tell us that when love dies we have to find another way of being alive.

T is for Trembling.

I said, Listen John, I don't want to hurt you, but I will. Our marriage is over.

W is for Woman.

She is sleeping, sorry. Call again tomorrow.

READING VIOLETTE LEDUC'S AUTOBIOGRAPHY, *LA BÂTARDE*

> At the age of five, of six, at the age of seven, I used to begin weeping sometimes without warning, simply for the sake of weeping, my eyes open wide to the sun, to the flowers . . . I wanted to feel an immense grief inside me and it came.

*L*a Bâtarde (1964) is a harsh title for an autobiography that is full of animals and children and plants and food and weather and girls falling in love with girls. It's true that Violette Leduc was the illegitimate daughter of a domestic servant who was seduced by the consumptive son of her employer, but to choose such a melodramatic and reductive title, 'The Bastard', tells us how hard it was for Leduc to escape from the way her mother described her, and in that description gave her daughter an internal crucifix on which to nail her life's story.

It's not surprising, then, that the furnace at the centre of Leduc's autobiography, and indeed all her writing, is stoked by her ambivalent steely-eyed mother, of whom she writes: 'You live in me as I lived in you.' Yet if the young Violette's tears spill from eyes that are open to the sun, the older Violette's words spill from the same place too. She is not blinded by her tears, nor are her eyes shut to the pleasures of being alive. Which is to say, Leduc was a writer very much in the world despite the distress she suffered all her life. What's more, she was a writer who was going to give maximum attention to the cause of her distress and create the kind of visceral language that often irritates hyperrational readers.

This is because Leduc experiences everything in her body:

As Isabelle lay crushed over my gaping heart I wanted to feel her enter it . . . She was giving me a lesson in humility. I grew frightened. I was a living being. I wasn't a statue.

She doesn't just (infamously) describe the physical sensations of sex between women, she describes the physical sensation of being unloved, the physical sensation of poverty, of snow, of war, of peacocks chuckling in a meadow – she is tuned in to the world with all her senses switched on. This is an extraordinary (and impossible) way of being in the world, but for Leduc it was ordinary. She is a writer who energizes whatever she gives her attention to, an orange shrivelling in the sun, an ink stain on a table, the white porcelain of a salad bowl. Leduc refused to bore herself. Nothing is decoratively arranged to suggest atmosphere or a sense of place or to set a scene. Everything on the page is there because the narrator perceives it as doing something.

Even as a young girl, Leduc knew she had to find her own

point to life. Her mother wanted her to be a Protestant, the religion of her absent father, but every time Violette tries to hear God, there is only absence. When she describes watching her beloved grandmother pray in church, Violette is shocked to realize that although she is sitting next to her, she has lost her. At that moment her grandmother is not there; she is in communion with somewhere else while Violette is doomed to be here, to be present, to be in this world. This is no small matter if you're poor, female, a bit bent, not that attractive (Simone de Beauvoir referred to her as 'the Ugly Woman'), and have nothing but your cunning and your talent to buy you bread. We know that Leduc's equivalent of the prayers that transported her grandmother elsewhere will be language. With words she not so much found the point to life as sharpened life to a point.

The French essayist Antonin Artaud, who was sometimes mad, wrote: 'I am a man who has lost his life and seeking to restore it to its place you hear the cries of a man remaking his life.' Is that why people write autobiographies? Are they attempting to remake their lives? *La Bâtarde* is not an attempt to remake Leduc's life, although there is no doubt that writing books was her salvation.

It is probably an attempt to stage her life and in so doing witness herself as its main performer – and what a performance. By the time she wrote her autobiography, Leduc had lived through two world wars, had intense and volatile affairs with women – the end of a love affair, she says, 'is the end of a tyranny' – been married and separated, written and published a few novels (in between lugging heavy suitcases of black-market butter and lamb from Normandy to sell to the rich in Paris), worked as a telephone operator, secretary, proof-reader and publicity writer. She also had a relationship with the writer Maurice Sachs. It was Sachs, a flamboyant homo-sexual, one-time reader for Gallimard, admirer of Apollinaire, Kant, Cocteau, Duras and Plato – not to mention fresh cream cakes, apple brandy and cigarettes – who encouraged Leduc to write instead of 'snivelling' all over him. Leduc portrays him as a sort of French Oscar Wilde, a man both bewildered and fascinated by women, who fills her with terror because of 'the gentleness in his eyes'. Leduc becomes infatuated with him because she has a 'passion for the impossible'. What kind of accommodation can be found, she wonders, with people we deeply love but who cannot give us all we want? What Sachs can do is tell her: 'Your unhappy childhood is beginning to bore me to distraction. This afternoon you will take your basket, a pen and an exercise-book, and you will go and sit under an apple tree. Then you will write down all the things you tell me.'

It was under that apple tree that she wrote the wonder-ful first line of her first novel, *L'Asphyxie*: 'My mother never gave me her hand.' Simone de Beauvoir read the manuscript and was so impressed she became Leduc's mentor, using her contacts to help get it published in post-Second World War Paris. When Leduc's editor, Jean-Jacques Pauvert, offered her 100,000 francs for the manuscript, she demanded the sum in cash, preferably in small bills.

By the time Leduc wrote *La Bâtarde*, she was going to return to themes she had written about before (her mother, the deprivations of her childhood, sexual passion, the erotics of everything, coffee, shoes, hair, landscape), but as a writer at the peak of her literary powers. In fact, she was uniquely placed to write an autobiography because she was a novelist who knew how to make the past and present seamlessly collide in one paragraph. Leduc also knew something that lesser writers do not know. She knew the past is not necessarily interesting. Eight lines into *La Bâtarde* she declares, 'There is no sustenance in the past.' This made me laugh, because I was on page one with 487 pages of 'the past' to go. She was clever, though. To observe so soon into her life story that there is no sustenance in the past is to give the past an edge. To make us curious about what the past lacks in sustenance for the narrator. What is the past anyway? What kind of place is it? Yes, it's a series of events that happened before now, but the past, like writing, is mostly a way of looking.

Leduc's cunning decision was to tell the reader that she is not unique, which is a relief – most people write autobiographies to persuade us that they are. She then goes on to wish she had been born a statue – presumably because if she were made from bronze rather than flesh she would not have to feel the painful things she is going to tell us about. Still on page one, she tells us she is sitting in the sunshine outside, surrounded by grapevines and hills, writing in an exercise-book. Suddenly she imagines her own birth. She is in a dark room. The doctor's scissors click as he separates the child from her mother: 'We are no longer the communicating vessels we were when she was carrying me.'

'Who is this Violette Leduc?' she asks. And then it's the

next day, she's picked some sweet peas, collected a feather, and is now writing in the woods, staring at the trunk of a chestnut tree. Every moment has breath and every breath pushes the narrative on to a surprising place, to somewhere that matters because it matters to Leduc. When she steals flowers, 'always blue', from a park, she connects the action to a perception. She says the flowers are her way of 'taking her mother's eyes back', by which I think she means she wants to find her mother's image in something beautiful. And when she is convalescing from an illness in the countryside, she writes: 'Whenever I looked round at the objects and furniture in the room I felt I was sitting on the point of a needle. So much cleanliness was repellent.' Her prose is kinetic and it is poetic, but it never collapses into poetry. In fact, her books are much more grounded in the realities and uncertainties of everyday life than some of her existentialist contemporaries.

Despite being acclaimed by Camus and Genet, Simone de Beauvoir and Sartre, Leduc's books certainly do not stand spine to spine with theirs in bookshops. Perhaps this is because nothing had taught her (or Genet) that life or literature was respectable. Literature for Leduc was not a comfortable sofa or a seminar room in a university – nor was it a place where flawed human beings undergo some sort of catharsis and emerge happy, whole, healed, miraculously cleansed of anger, lust and pain.

To declare there is no sustenance in the past is of course a half-lie. What sustained Leduc is that she wrote out her life with an audience in mind. It is for this reason she 'bit into the fruit' of her 'desolations' – that's what many writers do, and Leduc is no crazier than them for having the audacity to believe they might be interesting. I disagree with Beauvoir, astute as she is, when she describes 'the unflinching sincerity' of *La Bâtarde* as written 'as though there were no one listening'. Beauvoir certainly did not write her own books believing no one was listening to her, and she must have been aware that even in an uninhibited autobiography such as this one, there is no such thing as an absolutely true memory – all writing (except for diaries, but that too is debatable) is shaped with an audience in mind. Leduc, who addresses the reader throughout as 'Reader, my reader', felt more entitled to be listened to than perhaps Beauvoir unconsciously thought she should feel.

Violette Leduc had to spend a lifetime unlearning how to see the world as her mother saw it. Most of us choose to be less alert to the things that grieve us. This was just not possible for Leduc.

THE LADY AND THE
LITTLE FOX FUR

Violette Leduc's novels are a bit peculiar. Jean Genet was one of Leduc's early admirers, as were Simone de Beauvoir and Camus. According to Edmund White's autobiography *My Lives*, Genet and Leduc even made an amateur film together – a re-enactment of a baptism in which Genet, who was an orphan, played the child and Leduc the mother. Both writers were illegitimate, born at a time (Leduc in 1907) when such things mattered. The theatre of baptism with its narratives of belonging, of being ordained and claimed, must have been very potent to stage. The mind whirls at the thought of what they might have got up to – what a shame the film has been lost. If, as White points out, both Proust and Genet 'were dismantling all received ideas about the couple, manhood, love and sexual roles' I would include Leduc in the rearranging of the social and sexual scaffolding of her time. I don't think she set out to do this, it was just that her life wasn't quite bourgeois or stable enough to do anything else.

Leduc was aware that her grand themes – loneliness, humiliation, hunger, defeat, disappointment – are great comic subjects. Samuel Beckett knew this, too. It requires a sensibility that is totally unsentimental, a way of staring at life.

However, it is female love and desire that are Leduc's main subjects. She herself stated that she wanted to express 'as exactly as possible, as minutely as possible, the sensations of physical love'.

In *The Lady and the Little Fox Fur* it is the sensation of hunger, of loss of a future, of everyday connection to the rhythms of busy Parisian life that concerns the old lady of the title. 'She was breathing the oxygen meant for people who had spent their day working. To cry out that it was impossible to begin her life all over again would be useless.'

Leduc's starving old woman isn't really old by today's standards. Nevertheless, we are told she 'was handling her sixtieth year as lightly as we touch the lint when dressing a wound'. It is because Leduc profoundly understands how mysterious human beings are that her attention as a writer is always in an interesting place. Her old lady gazes at a calf's tongue in a butcher-shop window and asks herself, 'What was there on a calf's tongue?'

It reminds her of fine sand on the petals of a yellow rose, which makes her think of painting sunsets in her younger days. Her paintings were her equivalent of 'altars and sacred wafers'. Leduc does not sanitize and flatten a perception and make it more literal than it is, she accepts its own language. Life, like language, is coherent and incoherent. Leduc folds into the texture of her narrative the strange in-between bits of experience.

She is incapable of coming up with a boring sentence. A gushing sentence now and again, perhaps. But even that's quite exciting. Evelyn Waugh's definition of fiction as 'experience totally transformed' or Hanif Kureishi's astute observation in *My Ear at His Heart* that writing is often a substitute for experience, a kind of daydreaming, are fair enough, but not completely true for her. Writing, for Leduc, is a concentrated form of experiencing. She is a present-tense sort of writer, and like Virginia Woolf she records 'the atoms as they fall upon the mind'. When her old lady wakes up thirsty one summer morning in Paris, she wants to find an orange to suck. So she rummages in the bins and discovers a reeking fox fur in a box labelled tripe. Instead of an orange she had found 'a winter fur in summer'.

She picks it up and takes it home. What does she do with it?

'She kissed him, and then went on kissing him, from the tip of his muzzle to the tip of his brush. But her lips were cold as marble: in her mind these kisses were also an act of religious meditation.'

'You are really crazy, Violette,' I said out loud. And then I read the next three lines.

'She looked him up and down, then burst into her first fit of uncontrollable laughter: the amusement he filled her with was no less sincere than the love she felt for him.'

Literary provocateurs have always written rather peculiar books, and great publishers have always published them. As the old lady remarks at the end of this gentle, bitter-sweet novel, her 'world consisted of nothing but what she had invented'.

THE THINKER

For the artist Francis Upritchard

Am I due an upgrade on my phone? Can I survive on very little sleep? Am I lucky? How much stress can I endure? Am I still young? Do I have the energy to play with my smallest children? Shall I ban certain foods from the apartment? My third daughter loves dancing and debating. She thickens her eyebrows with a brown pencil. She will not make tea for the husbands of her older sisters. She is certainly tactless, but she does not fear men. Is she wise or foolish? Will she inherit my insomnia? Her body is bigger than my own. Is her femininity stronger than my masculinity and what does that even mean? Will I sink into mysticism and write a bestseller? Or will I sink into my suffering self (entombed in my hat) and write a pamphlet to achieve cheap fame? Is it time to make a will? If I leave the oldest son my animals (I have not named the monkeys, but I have never caged them), will he love them or beat them or give them away? Or should I bequeath him my bespoke suit, cut by a tailor in Gujarat? I would prefer all seventeen of my children to not eat the flesh of animals, but three of them suck marrow bones and one of them eats the trotter. I am not an extreme thinker. I have never shouted, 'God is dead' from the top of a mountain.

I am not looking for the abyss.

Is it looking for me?

Is pornography dulling my libido? Are there enough miles in my mind to walk the long road to enlightenment? Am I waiting like a discreet spy for new desires to surface? So far, vintage desires turn me on the most – hello, my old friends. Every new thought is a throne before it crashes to the ground. I am not a king. I am not a prince.

My mind is crammed with broken furniture.

I am pleased to have seen two antelopes resting in a star-lit field in Marfa, Texas. There is so much I want to see. There is so much I don't want to see. I don't want to open letters from the bank. Or from my first wife. Or from Helen or Samuel or Mastercard. What am I looking forward to? What? Something. What?

I like washing my ninth daughter's white plimsolls with a scrubbing brush and placing them on the radiator to dry. Is my mind a profoundly serious instrument? Am I too calm for an electrifying chase with someone, with something? Do I like the shape of my penis? Is there a shiver racing down my spine? Am I a magician or am I just stupefied from watering my crops while the rain falls?

Will I ever get round to making plans for the future or am

I too fragile for the dig? Am I willing to change? Am I original and contemporary or just good fun late at night? The news is encouraging for my football team. The players have prepared themselves mentally for a difficult match. One–nil so far.

Is the arrangement of ideas more important than the idea itself? Reason, Intention, Surfaces, Depths, Essences.

I am waiting for the fierce daughter with the eyebrows to return from watching films at her friend's house. We enjoy talking to each other. Her favourite philosopher is Simone Weil. Really, she is a much more interesting thinker than I am.

CHARISMA

Lynne Turner's job was to teach university staff how to communicate clearly. She wore a blue suit and told us that eye contact is important. She said, 'When you walk up to someone, you look them straight in the eye, shake their hand, tell them your name, and announce, "It's a pleasure to meet you."'

While she was saying this I thought about the film *Blade Runner*. I imagined Lynne Turner as a replicant who had learned how to be human in a workshop. I saw her sitting on a pink bedspread in her room, opening an envelope. She is four days old and she knows she only has a four-year lifespan.

In *Blade Runner* replicants are programmed with memories to make them more like humans – so in the envelope are some photographs to give Lynne Turner a forged history. The first photo is of her mother smiling in a yellow summer dress. The second is of a little girl called Lynne clasped in her mother's arms, their cheeks pressed against each other, and in the background a garden with a child's swing. The third photo is of eighteen-year-old Lynne sitting next to a young man on the big wheel in a fairground. Lynne Turner sits in her bedroom practising over and over how to say: 'The man on the big wheel was my first boyfriend, Mike. He broke my heart.'

Lynne Turner told us to get into pairs and work on what she called the Meet and Greet exercise. So I asked a professor in his late fifties, a gentle person, much loved by his students, if he'd be my Meet and Greet partner. His wife had died three months ago and his office was full of flowers. I looked into his sad blue eyes, shook his hand and said, 'My name is Deborah. It's a pleasure to meet you.'

I thought he'd laugh. We knew each other well, but he looked genuinely pleased to meet me and I was confused because I was acting and felt like I had tricked him. Then it was his turn. He walked slowly towards me, held out his hand, looked at my hair and said in a low voice, 'My name is . . . my name is . . . um . . . it's a pleasure to hold your hand.'

Lynne Turner asked us all to report back to her. I said, 'Roger communicated very well. He's definitely someone I'd like to meet and get to know.' 'Excellent,' said Lynne Turner in the voice she had learned in the first four days of her life. 'Could Professor Wilson please show us how he made eye contact with his partner.' So Roger, watched by everyone in the group, stood up and walked towards me. He was shaking and his hands were sweaty. This time he closed his blue eyes and just held on to my hand. The replicant Lynne Turner, whose eyes were made in a laboratory, frowned and wrote something down on her clipboard.

And I thought about the replicant Lynne Turner standing in the middle of a road alone in the rain. She takes out the creased faked photograph of a six-year-old girl in her mother's arms, and she stares at it for a long time. As the rain falls on her DNA, she practises saying, 'This is my mother. Her name is Elsa. She is a war correspondent and in great danger at the moment.'

'So,' said Lynne Turner, 'do you feel happy with the eye contact Professor Wilson made with you just then?'

I explained that eyes are like that, they open and close.

MONA LISA

Her hair looks uncared for under her hood. She probably has lice. I know she's too thin. If she took off her dress, you'd see her ribs. Her breath smells of sour milk. Her lips scare me. Her face is irradiated with light. I want to kiss her just under her mad right eye.

She says one day, when da Vinci was three years old, a bird flew in through the window and landed on his crib. It turned its back on him and stroked his lips with its tail feathers. The bird might have been the spirit of his father who abandoned him, then wrenched him away from his mother to live in his house.

Her voice sounds very foreign to me.

She says she's not unhappy or happy. She says she's all right. Today is all right and yesterday was all right.

I say, Mona Lisa, where were you born? No one knows who you are. She says, what sort of question is that? I was made in Leonardo da Vinci's head.

I can feel her breath under her dress.

ENSLAVED TO THE EVIL FLOWER OF FAME AS TOLD BY A DOG

(With thanks to Charles Baudelaire)

I have cultivated my hysteria with delight and terror; I have felt the wing of madness pass over my eyes and an orgy of words pour from my lips; I voice my lament with full ardour at the feet of writers who are nothing but beautiful prisoners enslaved to the evil flower of fame which like a log in the fireplace always smokes the room; my thoughts roam like syphilis amongst the wild boar and jasmine. I tell you I tell you I can barely conceive of any writer in whom there is not a longing for both oblivion and applause; my childhood is the bone that broke my teeth and from which I gnaw at shards of memory in the green grass by the lake where I compose my lament to recite (not Sundays) to beggars and pigeons; irony is my sister, my callous mother is cadence, my father haunts the drains, the moon is my hollow-cheeked dandy brother; I tell you I tell you once again, it is tedious to represent what exists, for everything that exists has already been written.

THE POSITION OF SPOONS

Surveillance is a creepy word. It suggests the cold, unblinking eye of various disembodied technologies. At least a human spy has eyes that cry. When I was twenty-six I lived on the upper floor of a house divided into two flats. The neighbour who lived on the lower floor was called Mr John. We shared a main front door and a tiny communal hallway to get to our respective flats. I did not know if John was his surname or his first name, and anyway, the mail addressed to his flat was inscribed with a different name altogether.

Mr John was already something of a mystery because his eyes were always hidden behind John Lennon-style purple-tinted spectacles. He was about fifty and had a shocking abundance of shoulder-length bone-white hair. It was as if the hormones that promote hair growth had accelerated rather than declined in his middle years. He told me he was a philosopher.

———

One morning, when we were both sorting out the post that flipped through the letterbox of the main door, I asked him what he thought of the German philosopher Friedrich Nietzsche's lament that he could not 'believe in a God who wants to be praised all the time'.

Mr John smiled. His lips were wide and thin and slightly purple like the lenses of his spectacles. 'Ah,' he said, 'but it is so encouraging to be praised. Perhaps Nietzsche was envious?' I thought that was a magnificent answer. No doubt about it, Mr John was a philosopher of the first order. The few other occasions we spoke in the hallway, he told me it was important to boil an egg for four and not five minutes and the spoon must be laid on the plate pointing towards the egg and not away from it.

At the time, I had a boyfriend who lived in Rome and who visited me every other weekend. When Matteo rang the bell on a Friday, I would run down the stairs to open the door, only to find that Mr John, unfailingly, always got there first.

It was as if my neighbour knew the exact time 'my Roman friend' would arrive and was as excited as I was to see him. The worst thing was that Matteo was excited to see Mr John, too. They would talk in the cramped hallway about all sorts of things – how to cook an artichoke, religious music, traffic problems in Rome and London – while I lurked on the stairs feeling like a gooseberry. Sometimes when we returned to the flat late at night from seeing a movie, Mr John would be hoovering the tiny patch of carpet in the hallway. On these occasions he wore pyjamas and a pair of laceless Oxford brogues. My neighbour never hoovered the hallway carpet when Matteo was not there.

Then, one Thursday evening, Mr John invited me into his flat for 'a glass of red and a plate of crackers and cheese'. I was curious because I had never seen the inside of his apartment. The only book in his living room was a copy of the *A–Z of London*. He gestured to me to sit on one of the two armchairs. When he was certain that I was sitting and not standing, he told me to please bear with him (as if he intuited he was unbearable) while he prepared the crackers and cheese.

As soon as he was out of the room, I got up from the armchair and walked over to the shelf above his fireplace to look at the postcards that were displayed there. One in particular had caught my eye. It was a blank white card, inked in black fountain pen with the words *miss you – miss you – miss you*. I knew it was an imitation of a letter that had been written by Man Ray to Lee Miller when they were having an affair in Paris, so I turned the card over to see who was missing Mr John.

It was addressed to me and not to him.

That night I called Matteo in Rome to thank him for his card.

He told me that he had been quite hurt that I'd said nothing about it. We decided that my neighbour, with his

89

all-too-human eyes hidden behind his tinted spectacles, was more of a voyeur than a spy.

Matteo was talking about Mr John so tenderly. I wondered if they might both be in love with each other? While he spoke I could hear an advertisement for a brand of washing-up liquid on his television in Rome. After a while, Matteo said, 'Most of all, I feel encouraged by the way he praises my route from Heathrow to your flat in the rush hour.'

THE MORTALITY PROJECT 2050

After Blade Runner

As the oldest female in this establishment for the vintage product (I was made in 1934), it is my greatest regret that I am wise and sane. Please give me a break and let in some fresh mad air. I have always thought the sane are over-rated and that I should have been designed with an occasional get-out clause. Alas, I am in full possession of all my marbles. If I had more courage I would roll a few of them into the dark night and see what happens in the morning. All the same, it is very hard to let go of all the known knowns. I know you are holding on tight to your own.

The most urgent thought preoccupying me here in my chair is that you might hold my unglamorous address against me, despite the minor chandelier. I am aware that a residence for the elderly has often been used as a setting to give voice to duller thoughts than my own. It is Christmas Eve. Green tinsel has been draped over the frames of all the pictures on the walls, mostly watercolours of cows grazing in the shires. The youngest carer (he tells me he was made in 1996) has wrapped a string of silver lametta around his wrists.

Every few hours I am brought tea, the liquid cosh that stops the English from speaking their minds. If you suspect my declaration of full sanity (with the seatbelt fastened) is a trick, let me tell you that would be incorrect. No, your wish to obsessively and compulsively disorder my mind and suggest it has been burgled is the wrong way to proceed. My mind is well made. However, it would be true to note that the mirror into which I gaze curiously, at what appears to be myself, presents to my own eyes a countenance that is more serene than myself. The gas is on full flame and the toast is burning in my lucid mind, despite it being assembled at a time when technology was less advanced.

It is precisely 16.00 GMT in the afternoon, 17.00 in Germany, 11.00 in New York, 23.00 in China – though I have not yet connected with Shanghai time. All day I have observed an assortment of relatives arrive with Yuletide gifts and cards. The cost of managing the mortality of their kin is immense. They do not say this out loud, but they are heard anyway. If only

I'd had the strength to escape to a rock on the edge of one of Earth's warmer oceans to soak up the sunlight and moonlight. I understand that my sanity would have been questioned had I been found wheezing under the stars, yet I wonder if lemon drizzle cake and tea is truly a less insane option.

These relatives know where their house keys are kept and remember where they parked the car. They know the day of the week and can name their prime minister. I have observed a senior manager (made in 1980) amongst them. His name is Thomas. He regards his wife as his cook and cleaner and needs an abundance of what he calls 'emotional support' at all times. Rumour has it that she has swapped their mattress stuffed with silk and cashmere for a floor in a shed in a forest in France. Every morning she cycles to a nearby coastal town to fish for small brown shrimp and weep away the years she wasted avoiding her wants. What a relief it would be if he unlocked his jaw and allowed it to speak freely to his staff (Team Zero Hours) in regard to their Christmas bonus. Might I help him with his first line?

I will write it now.

Alas, the nurse assigned to put me to bed has interrupted my script for Thomas's speech. Her blue eyes (made in 1974) are bright; her helmet of brown hair is her armour. The good thing is that her skin smells of onions. Her small, glossed lips are alive, like a water rat. The festive eyelashes glued to her upper eyelids suit her. Every time she moves nearer to me, my shoulders slump voluntarily.

'How are you today, Monica?' She sits near my knees and reaches for my hand.

'I am a vintage product, otherwise I would not be a resident in this establishment.'

'But you have your cat here with you,' she says consolingly.

'Indeed. But my cat (made in 2017) is young and shy and does not like to be spoken about out loud.'

The nurse slyly nudges my slice of lemon drizzle closer to her lively lips.

'You were something big in shipping – is that correct, Monica?'

'I was captain of my family's commercial vessel from the age of twenty,' I reply, reaching deep into my biographical data.

'The things you must have seen.' She widens her eyes in the manner of eyes that were made in 1974. 'Shall I wash you before you go to bed?'

'Please,' I wave my hand at the wallpaper that was made in 1963, 'ask me if I am afraid of dying and what kind of accommodation I have made with endless sanity.'

'Cheer up,' says the sane nurse.

'Since you ask,' I reply, 'I do have some terror of leaving the port for the final voyage out. It is not just a matter of never seeing a flower open again or my cat yawn for the last time. No, it is the erasure of the small victories in my existence that makes me reluctant to set sail. The times I dared to be bolder than my maker thought possible, those occasions in which I extended my own reach and flew closer to the moon.'

She nods humanely and tells me it is time.

'Time for what?'

'To rest,' she says. 'It's the big day tomorrow.'

I lift the blue blanket from my lap and hand it to the nurse while I raise my small but perfectly made body from the chair.

'Oh God! No!' she shouts as I detour from my vertical position and attempt to lower myself to the ground.

'Please stop that,' she pleads in plain and direct English. 'You'll never get up again. What are you doing?'

'I am taking the knee with the National Football League of America and with Stevie Wonder. Please hold my walking stick. Thank you.'

That night I met an angel with eyes that imperceptibly changed colour while we engaged in silent conversation using strange and beautiful hand gestures.

It is a silvery dawn. All is calm. All is bright.

WATERY THINGS

I have measured out my life with coffee spoons

—T. S. ELIOT, 'THE LOVE SONG OF J. ALFRED
PRUFROCK' (1915)

I have measured out my life with anchovies on buttered bread. It's all ha-ha eating anchovies in Hackney, oh yes, like a wind blowing in from Capri. I have measured out my life with whelks, mussels, clams, oysters, winkles and crab, but not the scallop, which is like eating the human earlobe.

I have measured out my life swimming in various rivers and lakes with dragonflies and humble ducks. But what about the plump carp basking in that weedy warm lake in August 2012? Oh no, that was not a good swim. There was a summer house painted green on the edge of that lake, and a rowing boat moored between two submerged trees. When I look back on that swim with the carp I can now see my life was about to change for ever. Why was the furniture smashed in the summer house? Why was the rowing boat tied to trees that were underwater? I know why. It was the end of one sort of life and the start of another. The fat carp were like the lies I had told myself to keep love alive.

Of all the oceans in which I have swum (including the Atlantic and Indian Oceans) the most inspiring is the Bay of Angels in Nice, the fifth biggest city in France. I have never glimpsed one single fish or felt it flick my feet in that stretch of water and often wonder why.

Swimming far out from shore that summer, then turning round to face the town, I saw the rooftops were covered in snow. At that moment I decided to write a novel called *Swimming Home*, set in the French Riviera.

Yet when I look at early drafts of this book, I can see it's not all ha-ha amongst the waves and cypress trees and casinos. There are notes I have made on war. The ambulances have no fuel, the hospitals have no water, a child is smuggled through a Polish forest in 1943. He will arrive safely in Whitechapel, London. This child is now an adult man and he is on holiday in the French Riviera. What happened to his mother, what happened to his father? He tells us they are night visitors, meaning he only meets them in dreams. He wonders if he will ever make it home. But where is home?

Also, in these early drafts, there is a quote from Sylvia Plath (*The Bell Jar*) in which a nurse says to an unhappy young woman, 'Show us how happy it makes you to write a poem.' In *Swimming Home* there is a fragile young woman with fierce intelligence and long red hair (her mother is a cleaner) who writes a poem. Maybe she's happy, maybe she's not. You will find her collecting pebbles on the beach of the Bay of Angels in a summer dress, the sky is always blue and the rooftops of the houses are carpeted in the seagulls that I first mistook for snow.

I have measured out my life with the sea urchins that have pierced my feet with their spines. I have now lost my fear of sea urchins. I don't know why. There are other fears I would prefer to lose, after all. I know they have to survive in the wilderness of the ocean; their cousins are the sea star and they can grow for centuries. There are sea urchins that are almost immortal, older than the mortal mothers and their mortal children fleeing from wars on boats that sometimes sink. Life is only worth living because we hope it will get better and we'll all get home safely. If we were to measure the love of mothers for their children with coffee spoons, there would never be enough spoons for that kind of love.

LETTER TO A STRANGER

For Philippa Beatrice, my mother

Dear Stranger,

As I write this letter my elderly mother is perhaps fatally unwell in hospital. I have to be careful because if she becomes well enough to read this, maybe I will feel totally foolish. She is not a stranger after all, though at the moment I don't think my mother currently feels like herself, as the saying goes.

I have found a few ways of coping.

It's a long walk to get to her ward. I walk down the corridors very fast like a soldier. I tell myself that if I slow down I might just turn around and run away. And I have made a rule that I will always look very smart when I visit my mother. So I take time putting on clothes I like wearing and doing my hair and it makes me laugh because I look like I'm going to an important meeting with a lot at stake. But this is an important meeting and there is a lot at stake.

Yesterday I was wearing a red dress and boots and did the usual soldier walk to the ward, clip clop clip. I can see why armies practise the art of marching. It resembles a steady heartbeat even if we are scared and our hearts are going berserk. When I enter the ward, I change the metabolism of that pace, walk softly, slowly.

I always sit on my mother's bed rather than on the bulky visitor's chair which is arranged at some distance from the bed with a table between us. No matter how unwell she is, I always say to her, 'Move up,' and though it is physically tricky (tubes attached to her body), she does, she makes a space for me. It is the most subtle of movements. The human endeavour it has taken to make that space is immense. Sometimes it's just two centimetres, but to me it is as vast as a night sky crowded with stars.

I bought her a radio and some headphones and started to put them together. The earpieces were massive, the size of two small black kittens. I placed them on the skull of her head while I tuned the radio to a programme I thought she would like. While she listened I perched in the space she had made for me and put some moisturizer on her lips, which get dry in hospital.

Now and again she lifted her hand to touch the red material of my dress. After a while she said, 'Crows have brains that are as big as a gorilla's. They can recognize people, they have a memory.'

I knew this information was from the programme she was listening to. I was pleased she was surprised. I didn't know that about crows either. After a while I left her to take my teenage daughter out for her favourite lunch – jerk chicken with rice and peas. That was Sunday. It wasn't the best or the worst day. This is not a life-affirming letter, it's just about a few moments in a bad situation.

I don't have a moral position on happiness. We have to find our own point to life, even if it's to learn something new about crows. All the same, I would give anything to hear my mother tell me again about the pleasure of red peppers and anchovies and to hear her laugh loudly (or softly), and to mean it.

X = FREEDOM

For Meret Oppenheim (1913–85)

Become an artist, Meret
Why don't you?
No one will give you freedom
You have to take it

That's what you said

We do have to take it
I do take it
I'm writing to you in my Berlin hotel
On book tour, away from home

And now I'm in Hamburg
Where it gently rains
On the stall selling pretzels

THE POSITION OF SPOONS

Rolls and sticks
Soft and hard

We have to look outwards
At the view
And inwards to find a point of view

Every day
In every century

It's a long view

What can I see now in this café
On a rooftop in Barcelona?
Standing tall on the dome of a church
A marble statue of the Mother of Jesus
Eyes lowered
Buenos dias, Mary

Become an artist, Meret
You're eighteen now
It's 1932
Why don't you live in Paris?

You take a room at Hotel Odessa in Montparnasse
Odessa is in Ukraine on the north-western shores of the
    Black Sea
The grain port to the world

You write letters home:
Mom, please send me a pillow and linen
And money
You drink absinthe and make twelve drawings
You make a sculpture of Giacometti's ear
From marzipan
A paste of almonds, sugar, honey

(You were extremely Swiss
in your loyalties, it has been noted)

Later, you will cast the ear in bronze

You walk on the edge of high buildings in Paris
Maybe it's a death wish for Jung to think about in his Swiss
    residence
Or your dangerous walk is just for the view
A point of view

You hold your sculpture of Giacometti's ear to the French sky

Très chère, Meret
I hear you
The ear collects sound waves
Across all of time

Cézanne's apples, oranges, onions
Baudelaire's wine, opium, hashish
Rimbaud's brawling and tears

THE POSITION OF SPOONS

You are loyal to the idea that dreams and reality
Come from the same unconscious

I am listening, Meret

You do not want to be a female artist
You want to be an artist
You will struggle with this
As we all do
As I do

'Women are not goddesses, not fairies, not
    sphinxes
All these are the projections of men,' you say.
I am listening here in Barcelona

You are a cup and you are a beast
You are a table and you are a bird
You are a white stiletto and you are meat

You are saying (not in these words)
Imagination is not he or she
You are saying
Leave me alone

Take your hands off me
I will create myself

You are saying

A glove has pulsating veins
Thoughts reside like bees in a hive
A boot is a lover: tied, untied
It does forbidden things in the night
Here is my gaze
This is how I look
This is what I am looking at
Make of it what you will

And what was made of it?
Meret?

You say your voice will be drowned in fur
A gazelle has ripped out your tongue

After you return to Basel in 1936
You will not be exhibited
For eighteen years
Turns out you are a female artist after all

And what of beauty?
Immense beauty like yours
Long and lean for Man Ray's camera
What of love?
Desire?

Max Ernst described you:
'That woman is a sandwich stuffed with marble.
You have to be careful not to break your teeth when
You bite into her.'

I am laughing with the olives from Andalusia
Bien sûr, Meret
You could not be shadow
To a famous male artist
Twenty years older than you
I understand

It's not an easy understanding
It's hard like marble

I do know this
I have lived this

Freedom is hard like marble

Your *Stone Woman* (1938)
A female body half in/half out of water
Only the feet are flesh

Sometimes we live like this
Hard soft
Liquid solid

You know this
We are not born a woman, we become one

We are not born from marble
We become it

Good morning, Mary

Good morning, Leonora, Lee, Dorothea, Claude, Dora
Remedios, Louise, Leonor, Valentine
Good morning to Lois Mailou Jones in her Paris studio

Here on the rooftop café in Barcelona
Two people are whispering in the corner
To have sex is like killing someone, they agree
Do they mean physically
Philosophically
Or is it existential murder?
I want to know

Meret, I think you would be interested, too

Shall we melt raclette on potatoes?
Shall we smoke a cigarette?
Shall we crack hazelnuts and get to the point?

It is hard to find a form for freedom
Deep, light, unstable, ageless
Shifting, raw, slippery, lonely

I am listening, Meret.

SEDUCTION AND BETRAYAL

Elizabeth Hardwick is one of the world's most valuable essayists and literary critics. That is to say, these essays are of value to anyone interested in the ways in which women are made present in literature. In *Seduction and Betrayal*, readers are treated to the full reach of Hardwick's deep intelligence, a hard, glinting, sophisticated, switched-on intelligence. She understands what is at stake in literature, especially when talented women write it.

For a female writer to risk stepping centre stage in life and on the page will always mean she has transgressed from the societally sanctified role of being a minor player, lurking behind the velvet curtains (less exposing) in order to assist, flatter, dedicate her life to the male world and its undermining arrangements. Hardwick has no interest in flattery, nor in faux solidarity with female writers. She cuts to the chase, offers her grateful readers new dimensions as to how literature is made and what it costs to make it. Hardwick is a shockingly astute reader, yet she never lets literary theory get in the way of the currents of life that blow into the writing itself. Her sentences are subversively beautiful for exactly this reason.

In an interview with *Paris Review* (issue 87), Hardwick is keen to point out that she does not write essays 'to give a résumé of the plots'. Of the action of reading itself, she has this to say:

> You begin to see all sorts of not quite expressed things, to make connections, sometimes to feel you have discovered or felt certain things the author may not have been entirely conscious of. It's a sort of creative or 'possessed' reading and that is why I think even the most technical of critics do the same thing, by their means making quite mysterious discoveries. But as I said, the text is always the first thing. It has the real claim on you, of course.

Hardwick's essay on the Brontë sisters is invigorating, still contemporary in its analysis of what it takes for women to own their talent without hurting the feelings of the men in their lives. She is the kind of critic who thinks it important to tell us that their reverend father was a failed writer and that the Brontë sisters kept news of their literary success secret from their brother. Why?

They did not wish to rub Branwell's nose in his own failure as an artist.

She quotes from Charlotte's letters: 'My unhappy brother

never knew what his sisters had done in literature – he was not aware that they had ever published a line. We could not tell him of our efforts for fear of causing him too deep a pang of remorse for his own time misspent, and talents misapplied.' What would it take for Branwell to actually have congratulated the sisters who cared for him? Here is Hardwick on this matter: 'It is only by accident that we know about people like Branwell who seemed destined for the arts, unable to work at anything else, and yet have not the talent, the tenacity, or the discipline to make any kind of sustained creative effort.'

Perhaps it takes an American writer to shake some of the dust off the Brontë heritage industry, to gaze without sentimentality, but with full admiration, at how women such as the Brontës prevailed, despite the patriarchal arrangements that beat them down, crushed their hopes for independence, held them back, shortened their lives. Hardwick, born in Kentucky, a long way from the wild Yorkshire moors as re-imagined by Emily Brontë, writes, '*Wuthering Heights* has a sustained brilliance and originality we hardly know how to account for.' Hardwick does account for it though: she gives us a new view of this strangely brilliant novel, and she is not interested in the bonnets or the length of the Brontë sisters' skirts. 'They are very serious, wounded, longing women, conscious of all the romance of literature and of their own fragility and suffering. They were serious about the threatening character of real life.'

Yet as she points out, if they were quiet and repressed in life, 'their readers were immediately aware of a disturbing undercurrent of sexual fantasy. Loneliness and melancholy seemed to alternate in their feelings with an unusual energy and ambition.'

When it comes to Charlotte Brontë, Hardwick cuts to the heart of the matter, and she cuts deep. She shocks with the truth: it runs like blood through her every sentence.

> How to live without love, without security? Hardly any other Victorian woman had thought as much about this as Charlotte Brontë. The large, gaping flaws in the construction of the stories – mad wives in the attic, strange apparitions in Belgium – are a representation of the life she could not face; these gothic subterfuges represent the mind at breaking point, frantic to find a way out. If the flaws are only to be attributed to the practice of popular fiction of the time, we cannot then explain the large amount of genuine feeling that goes into them. They stand for the hidden wishes of an intolerable life.

If Hardwick elevates Emily as the sister who is the literary genius, she ends with this thought on all their lives: 'We are astonished by what they could *not* endure.'

The essay titled 'Amateurs' flips the Branwell problem and looks at the life of Dorothy Wordsworth, a life devoted and dedicated to her much more talented brother. Perhaps Branwell fared better than virtuous Dorothy by getting blind drunk, rollicking through town and being helpless enough to solicit the care of his sisters. Hardwick sees this somewhat abject, controlling sister as resembling a heroine in a Brontë novel. 'There was always something peculiar about Dorothy Wordsworth; she is spoken of as having "wild lights in her eyes".'

Dorothy Wordsworth is not a character in a novel though. In a witty aside, Hardwick tells us that Dorothy lives Wordsworth's 'life to the full'. It costs her. When she is almost sixty she goes mad. Yet in Hardwick's view, 'she is always a little bit mad and in nothing more so than in her fanatic devotion to her brother.'

The British have never liked their avant-gardists much, alas, and perhaps Hardwick feels the same. She is dismissive of the lifestyle of Bloomsbury and its associates. 'The arrangements of Bloomsbury, shored up by stout logs of self-regard, are insular in the extreme.'

She is amused and bemused by the way they eschewed monogamy and swapped sexual partners. I'm sure that Dora Russell would have enjoyed Hardwick's quip on her randy philosopher husband: 'Even Bertrand Russell astonishes with his passionless copulations, his mastery of forgetfulness, his sliding in and out of relationships and marriages as if they were a pair of trousers.'

All the same, I can't see how Vanessa Bell could have had children and managed to paint every day if she had lived within the patriarchal constraints of her time. And never would I agree with Hardwick on the worth of Virginia Woolf's literature: 'The aestheticism of Bloomsbury, "the androgyny", if you will, lies at the root of Virginia Woolf's narrowness. It imprisons her in a femininity, as a writer at least, instead of acting as a way of bringing the masculine and feminine into a whole.' I am not obliged to agree, and I certainly don't agree, but I appreciate the provocation.

The essay on Sylvia Plath is devastating, as it should be. The *Ariel* poems are devastating.

I can't see why a serious critic, someone whose thoughts I would value, might offer a lofty, mocking, disengaged tone to write about these poems. No, Hardwick rises to the devastating task, as she knew she must. She tells us that Plath has the 'rarity of being, in her work at least, never a "nice person"'. Plath's luminous mastery as a poet, at the time of writing *Ariel*, is described by Hardwick, like this: 'In the last freezing months of her life she was visited, like some waiting stigmatist, by an almost hallucinating creativity – the astonishing poems in *Ariel* and in a later volume called *Winter Trees*.' When Plath died, 'she was alone, exhausted from writing, miserable – but triumphant too, achieved, defined and defiant.'

The same cannot be said of Zelda Fitzgerald's attempt to write and to live meaningfully. She took up ballet lessons later in her marriage. When she became mentally fragile, she was forbidden to dance and write, the two activities that made her feel well. Hardwick sees Zelda's life as 'buried beneath the ground, covered over by the desperate violets of Scott Fitzgerald's memories'. These sweet, cloying, metaphorical flowers were a cover-up for all that could not be said – perhaps all that Zelda was forbidden to say herself.

Seduction and Betrayal interrogates how language is put

together in the full force of life's vicissitudes – poverty, loss, madness, defiance. Hardwick makes new plots from old plots and always has something exciting to bring to the table. The gift of her attention is enough to make anyone want to write magnificently.

LEMONS AT MY TABLE

It has often occurred to me that the eggs and lemons in my kitchen are the most beautiful things in my home. I see no reason to hide them in the fridge and instead place them centre stage in a bowl on my dining table.

They are sculptures, each of them a one-off, despite their similarity in form and colour. Eggs have the added uncanny allure of being an artwork that is made inside the body of a hen. Freud, who disliked eating chicken, apparently once shouted, 'Let the chickens live and lay eggs.' I agree, though admit that I don't always listen to Freud and sometimes roast a chicken, usually with a lemon stuffed inside it.

It's uplifting to glance at a bowl of sunny lemons with their startling palette of yellows on a cold British winter morning. I have been lucky enough in my life to have spent summers walking down a mountain to a beach in Majorca through lemon orchards that eventually lead to the sea. By the end of summer, many of the lemons have fallen to the ground and lie scattered below the trees. I often think about this walk when I buy a miserable lemon from my local London corner shop in February. Shivering in the rain, I know that the lemon (and I) would rather be in that orchard, and that we are both migrants.

When I first came to England from Africa, age nine, my new best friend brought lemon curd sandwiches to school. I had never heard of such an exotic thing as lemon curd. The bread was white and soft with a thin stripe of the sweet yellow paste just visible between the slices. My friend came from a religious Christian family and always said grace before she ate her packed lunch. For a while, I associated lemon curd with a higher spiritual force, as if it were a substance somehow entwined with God.

At Christmas my daughters pierce lemons with cloves and we decorate the table with them for the feast. In their teenage years, they squeezed lemon juice on to their hair, believing it would 'bring out the highlights'. I'm not sure it did, but the juice was youthful, like them. They were excited to think their hair might develop new, unknown dimensions, in the same way that I was always excited to see how photographs were going to develop in the dark rooms of my generation. The taste and fragrance of lemon rind has a totally different mood from its juice: the oil in the skin, particularly when it is used as a 'twist' for a dry vodka martini, is intense, deep, flamboyant, serene, while the juice is perhaps slightly neurotic.

I am staring at the bowl of unwaxed lemons on my table right now. Wax is used to preserve the freshness of their skin and protect them in transit, but as I mostly use their zest, these are the lemons of my choice. Given the beauty of their form, I am not surprised they have historically been muses and models for many famous artists. Sometimes a lemon has had to take off its peel when posing for a still life, but it is more usual to see it resting on a plate, happy in its own skin.

HOPE MIRRLEES

PARIS: A POEM

. . . behind the ramparts of the Louvre

Freud has dredged the river and, grinning horribly,
waves his garbage in a glare of electricity.

> Taxis,
> Taxis,
> Taxis,
> They moan and yell and squeak

If modernism was the language that lit up the early twentieth century, it seems to me that Hope Mirrlees, aged
twenty-six, stepped into that light and flipped a switch of her
own. In 1919, when she set about writing the immersive poly-
phonic adventure of a day and night walking through post-
war Paris just after the Armistice, it's possible that Mirrlees, in
finding a form for the multiple impressions that eventually became *Paris: A Poem*, might even have astounded herself with
her own audacity. It is also a valuable historical document of a
European city haunted by the spectres of the war dead while
the bereaved living go about their day.

No wonder Virginia and Leonard Woolf, who had set up the Hogarth Press together, were keen to publish *Paris: A Poem* in 1920. Virginia Woolf even sewed by hand the 175 copies they printed in their English home. It's exciting to think of the endeavour it must have taken to visually lay out and print the typographical effects and roaming line breaks – it's as if the poem itself is strolling through the May day demonstrations and street singers, pausing to notice a red stud in the buttonhole of a gentleman's frock coat in Gambetta, then moving on to gaze at statues of nymphs with 'soft mouths'. Virginia Woolf must have enjoyed this splash of cosmopolitan life as their printing press (bought second-hand in 1917 for £41) rolled off the pages of Mirrlees's poem in their house in Richmond, then in Surrey – not known for its avant-garde sensibility.

> The sky is apricot;
> Against it there pass
> Across the Pont Solférino
> Fiacres and little people all black,

We could linger for a while to imagine this publishing moment at Hogarth House in post-war Britain. Perhaps the starlings were singing in the English mist, vegetables were being boiled to death in the kitchen, while in another room Mirrlees brought news of lesbian nightclub 'gurls', advertisements in the Métro for Dubonnet, cigarette papers and shoe polish – meanwhile the Seine, 'old egoist', is making its way to the sea and the ghosts of the dead mingle with children riding fairground horses.

I can see Virginia being called to the table while rain drips in the garden, trapped (as she saw it) in sedate Richmond, trying not to go mad again (rage at patriarchy that refused to give her an education), glancing at these words:

> It is pleasant to sit on the Grands Boulevards –
>> They smell of
>> Cloacae
>> Hot indiarubber
>> Poudre de riz
>> Algerian tobacco

It's possible that Mirrlees was influenced by the concrete poetry of Apollinaire (she might have read his *Calligrammes* of 1918) and would never again, in her other writing, rise to the same level of linguistic bravado she achieved on that long walk in 1919. If this is my own view, it can be contested, and that is how it should be. Yet I believe it only gives *Paris* more allure. When Baudelaire and Rimbaud flâneured the same city, they were societally able to loiter in public space and observe metropolitan life with more ease and entitlement than Mirrlees could do – after all, female streetwalkers were apparently prostitutes and not poets. Born in Kent, raised in Scotland, educated in London but now living in Paris with her partner the classicist Jane Harrison, Mirrlees had to find a form to evoke simultaneous experience in the way that cubism had created a visual language to capture multiple points of view. At times she slows everything down and paints the mood of the city in three simple short lines:

> The wicked April moon
> The silence of *la grève*
> Rain

As the writer Francesca Wade points out in *Square Haunting* (2020), her superb literary history of five extraordinary women living in London between the wars (in which you will meet Hope Mirrlees, Virginia Woolf and Jane Harrison all figuring out how to find a way of living that allows them to write and love freely), the British were never that keen on modernism. When the work of Matisse, Van Gogh, Gauguin and Cézanne was exhibited in London in 1910, Wade tells us how Virginia Woolf recorded the way it threw critics into 'paroxysms of rage and laughter'. Ten years later, when Mirrlees's poem was published, this atmosphere of cultural conservatism still prevailed. If there were not many readers for her unique early stretch of female modernist writing, it certainly paved the way for T. S. Eliot's *The Waste Land*, published in 1922.

My wish for the 26-year-old Mirrlees is that she had been encouraged to fly higher and to continue with some of the innovations she had started to make manifest in *Paris: A Poem*.

INTRODUCTION TO
THE INSEPARABLES BY
SIMONE DE BEAUVOIR

(TRANSLATED BY LAUREN ELKIN)

In every decade of my life since my twenties, I have been awed, confused, intrigued and inspired by Beauvoir's attempt to live with meaning, pleasure and purpose. 'Be loved, be admired, be necessary; be somebody,' she insisted in her autobiography *Memoirs of a Dutiful Daughter*.

The act of her writing what has now been titled *The Inseparables* cannot be separated from this epic endeavour. It is a valuable part of the long conversation that Beauvoir's many books have begun with old and new readers.

After she won the Goncourt Prize for the immense reach of *The Mandarins*, I can see it must have been appealing for Beauvoir to write an intimate novella. *The Inseparables* once again returns to her friendship (from the age of nine) with

Élisabeth Lacoin, nicknamed Zaza. Beauvoir's readers know that this friendship had long haunted her, not only in her books, but in her dreams.

In my view she never quite managed to write up the spectre of Zaza entirely convincingly, which is why she kept returning to try and catch her on the page. Maybe this is because her own fierce desire for Lacoin/Zaza to have finally risked claiming the life she deserved might have been stronger than Zaza's own desire to risk all she would lose in doing so: God, her family, bourgeois respectability.

Given childhood is the beginning of everything we feel most deeply, it is not surprising that Beauvoir's strong feelings and hopes for Élisabeth Lacoin were also the beginning of her political education.

At the time they were at school together, women could not vote, were coerced into marriage and societally encouraged to accept an existence that mostly involved servicing the needs of their future husbands and children.

So, what sort of girl was Élisabeth Lacoin? Her avatar in *The Inseparables* is named Andrée, Beauvoir is Sylvie.

In her very first encounter at a private Catholic school with Sylvie, new pupil Andrée announces she was 'burned alive' while cooking potatoes at a campfire. Her dress caught alight and her right thigh was 'grilled to the bone'. Andrée's bold and playful tone is captured perfectly in Lauren Elkin's translation from the French. Elkin skilfully manages to convey, in pared-down prose, Andrée's beguiling sensibility and the ways in which Sylvie is enraptured by her forthright manner: her confidence, her cartwheels, her talent for literature, playing the violin, riding a horse, mimicking teachers. Sylvie is bored and intellectually lonely, so meeting this clever, devout, but irreverent girl, changes her life. Sylvie tells us, 'Nothing so interesting had ever happened to me. It suddenly seemed as if nothing had ever happened to me at all.'

Andrée tends to say tragic things in a way that deliberately does not invite sympathy. This is a clever narrative trick on Beauvoir's part. It means that Sylvie can do all the feeling for Andrée. She observes that her new friend does not speak to teachers in a humble manner, nor is she discourteous. In fact, she tells the female teacher that she is not intimidated by her. Why is that? It's not because she is above being intimidated, it's just that the teacher is not intimidating.

There is much that society will throw at Andrée to intimidate and flatten her, not least religion and her desire to not disappoint her controlling, conservative mother. And to make life as complicated as it actually is – which novelists must do – Andrée loves her mother. Sylvie can jealously see that all other attachments are not as important to her friend. How can she compete with this maternal bond, even usurp it?

When Sylvie, who hates needlework, goes to great effort to sew Andrée a silk bag for her thirteenth-birthday present, she suddenly realizes her friend's mother, Madame Gallard, doesn't like her any more. Beauvoir hints that this mother understands that the sewing of the silk bag was a labour of love, and disapproves of these strong feelings for her daughter.

Sylvie falls in love with Andrée's mind. Obviously, her

manner and liveliness make her body attractive too. Yet, this kind of cerebral love is subversive because for Beauvoir's generation (she was born in 1908) the minds of girls and women were not what made them valuable. The girls have long conversations together. They continue talking for twelve years.

'We could lose ourselves for hours in discussions of property, justice and equality. We had zero respect for our teachers' opinions, and our parents' ideas didn't satisfy us either.'

The talking cure between Andrée and Sylvie is nothing less than a revolution at a time when girls and women were encouraged to keep their thoughts to themselves. 'They teach you in catechism to respect your body. So selling your body in marriage must be as bad as selling it on the street,' Andrée says.

The enigma of female friendship that is as intense as a love affair, but that is not sexually expressed, or even particularly repressed, is always an interesting subject. Yet, while Sylvie, who is now a teenager, listens to Andrée speak of her passion for her male cousin – she has taken up kissing him and now smokes Gauloises – she also owns her emotional turbulence.

'I suddenly understood, in a joyful stupor, that the empty feeling in my heart, the mournful quality of my days, had but one cause: Andrée's absence. Life without her would be death.'

Sylvie is endearingly vulnerable because she risks loving Andrée – and of course, any kind of love involves a fair dose of fantasy, projection, imagination. The idolized subject of her affection does not reciprocate the strength of her feelings, nor does she believe herself to be lovable. Meanwhile, Andrée's older sister, Malou, is being groomed for marriage with 'stupid and ugly' male suitors.

Madame Gallard's message to her daughters is clear: 'Join a convent or get a husband; remaining unmarried is not a vocation.'

What I find most touching in *The Inseparables* is the description of Sylvie losing her faith. In various interviews, Beauvoir has described the experience of suddenly not believing in God as 'a kind of awareness'. Literature would eventually take the place of religion in her life and fill the void of an evaporated God.

When Sylvie is fourteen she realizes during confession with the school priest that her relationship with God is changing. 'I don't believe in God! I said to myself . . . The truth of it stunned me for a moment: I didn't believe in God.'

The priest picks up on this new mood and chastises her.

'I have been told that my little Sylvie is not the same girl she was,' said the voice. 'It seems she has become distracted, disobedient, and insolent.'

Instead of being apologetic, Sylvie becomes rebellious. With her caustic wit, Beauvoir tells us that Sylvie was more shaken by her new lack of respect for this priest than by the man who had recently flashed her on the métro.

Andrée asks Sylvie an important question.

'If you don't believe in God, how can you bear to be alive?'

Sylvie replies, 'But I love being alive.'

Does Andrée love being alive? We know that she was nearly burned alive as a young girl. At her family's country house, to which Sylvie is invited, Andrée pushes herself so perilously high on a swing that Sylvie fears it will topple over. She wonders anxiously if 'something had broken inside her mind, and she couldn't stop'.

When she is again in dispute with her harassing mother and wishes to get out of a tedious family engagement, Andrée cuts a deep wound into her foot with an axe while chopping wood.

> Suddenly someone cried out. The voice was Andrée's.
> I ran to the woodshed. Madame Gallard was leaning over her; Andrée was lying in the sawdust, bleeding from her foot; the edge of the axe was stained red.

When Andrée opens her eyes, she says, 'The axe got away from me!'

In the fairy tale 'The Red Shoes' by Hans Christian Andersen, the female protagonist wears a beloved pair of red shoes to church. She is told that it is improper to do so, but she cannot resist. To cure her vanity, a magic spell is cast, in which, not only can she never take off her red shoes, but she is doomed to dance non-stop in them for ever. Eventually, she finds an executioner and asks him to chop off her feet. He obliges, but her amputated feet continue to dance of their own accord. To quote Beauvoir, it is as if 'something had broken in her mind and she couldn't stop'. Is Andrée her own executioner?

She needs to use the axe to separate from her mother,

but instead turns it on herself. This scene is a prelude to what Beauvoir saw as the execution of Andrée Gallard by society.

By the time they study together for their exams at the Sorbonne, Andrée begins a romance with a fellow student, Pascal Blondel, the avatar for the extraordinary phenomenologist Maurice Merleau-Ponty. This relationship is disapproved of by her parents, who are keen to marry off their clever daughter. When Sylvie and Andrée meet for tea to discuss this forbidden (chaste) romance, Sylvie observes: 'All around me perfumed women ate cake and talked about the cost of living. From the day she was born, Andrée was fated to join them. But she was nothing like them.'

Andrée does not join them. She dies from meningitis instead, broken-hearted and defeated. Beauvoir saw her death as nothing less than murder. At the funeral, as Madame Gallard sobs, while her husband says, 'We have been but instruments in the hands of God,' Sylvie places three red roses amongst the white roses heaped on her coffin, red as the blood that dripped from the axe. If she had always secretly thought that 'Andrée was one of those prodigies about whom, later on, books would be written', she was correct.

Simone de Beauvoir would write it.

PAULA REGO

SHE DOESN'T WANT IT

The desires and appetites of the beguiling girls and women at the centre of Rego's visual narratives radically return to her protagonists their mystery and subjectivity. This is not a small matter. It is one of the many reasons why the emotional and imaginative reach of Rego's startling visual language has such vitality and contemporary resonance. If some of her recurring themes are childhood, coming of age, family entanglements, enchantment, seduction, betrayal, submission and metamorphosis, they often play out in heightened domestic interior spaces. The furniture is as animated and psychologically charged as her protagonists.

It is a wonder to think of the glamorous young artist, Maria Paula Figueiroa Rego, born in Lisbon in 1935, at work under England's grey sky at the Slade School in 1950s Bloomsbury. Although she had been partly educated in Britain and encouraged to be an artist by her anglophile, anti-fascist father, what was she going to do with all that was already laid down inside her, from childhood to her teenage years in Portugal? Poetry, songs, folklore, a whole other palette and language, but most significantly the violence of Salazar's repressive right-wing dictatorship.

In a sense, all of Rego's art over the decades has obliquely or overtly argued with the motto that represented the values of Salazar's authoritarian military regime: *Deus, Pátria e Família*. If girls and women were idealized as virgins, wives and mothers serving God, the Fatherland and Family, Rego had other stories to tell (in paint, pastel, collage and sculpture) about our purpose in life. Magical, perplexing, furious stories, in which an everyday chore, such as polishing a boot, could look both heartbreaking and sinister.

There is rarely one fixed meaning in any image. Rego's artfulness is to suggest a moment of change or contemplation, or to offer simultaneous narratives to fracture time. This can be seen in the multiple storylines of the Misericordia series (2001), inspired by the writings of the nineteenth-century Spanish novelist Benito Pérez Galdós. Her gaze on the female body in all phases of life is brutally true and endearingly tender, in this case the bare-bottomed old women being helped to the bathroom or to get dressed, with the detail of a smart handbag (perhaps a whole abandoned life inside it) resting tragically on a cupboard.

It has been suggested by Rego that to create art is to liberate desire and all its consequences. 'Everything's erotic because work itself is erotic,' she has commented. 'Doing work, that is to say, drawing, is an erotic activity.' She is particularly astute on the legend of girlhood and its erotic charge.

If some of us are nasty and some of us are nice, mostly we are a mix of both, as in *Sophia's Friends* (2017). The pretty pastel colours contrast with the fierce, secret, interior lives of these three girls, while the power relations between them are inflamed with Rego's droll humour. The arm of the smallest girl, wearing a white dress, is being grasped by the older, mischievously sadistic girl, who warily looks out at us, as if she has been caught rough handling her friend. Yet it is the last of this trio, the girl with neat plaits who sits on the end of the prim, upholstered bench, who gives this composition its pathos. Her eyes are closed, maybe to zone out of the conflict and dream herself elsewhere.

As in the fairy tales and nursery rhymes that have long inspired her work, Rego has personified people as animals, or hybrids of both. *Girl on a Large Armchair* (2000) brings back the predatory dog that appears in much of her work.

It seems to have been summoned by the woman who is seated on an armchair, which also resembles a kind of throne. Her hands rest assertively on her thighs, muscular legs slightly apart, yet, as ever with Rego, it is also her thoughts that animate her body. Fading sunflowers peer over her left shoulder. Hiding under the chair is a girl, a child, and staring at her is the dog, straining on his hind legs as he lowers himself towards her. Paws outstretched, he lifts up the blanket under which she lies. The dog seems ravenous, the girl looks bemused. Some sort of protective creature lies with her under the blanket. It is as if the woman on the chair is thinking about her younger self, reminiscing about a moment of being seduced, pawed, eaten alive – or perhaps she will eat the dog herself.

This memory, or story, continues with *Convulsion IV* (2000), also embodied with wax crayon and watercolour, in which two realities take place simultaneously. The woman in the armchair is spitting blood while another woman, barefoot, lies flat out at her feet.

Rego's pencil is very playful in *She Doesn't Want It* (2007). A smiling young female protagonist, who looks a little like a fairy-tale princess, seems to be offering a limb to a seated scowling woman. We are not sure what it is she doesn't want or what exactly is being offered. It is the refusal that captures our curiosity. If she is saying no to whatever it is she is supposed to want, it is not just refusal, it is protest. This is echoed in *Sick of It All* (2013), for which Rego returns to delicate watercolour. A moody older woman, wearing a sensual red dress, sits on a mass of purple that is vaguely intestinal – as if her insides are pouring out of her body. The ambience is both turbulent and serene. Like all good storytellers, the artist leaves it to the viewer to step into the image and improvise with its meanings.

There is a quote by Jacques Lacan that gets somewhere close to the experience of looking at a Rego drawing: 'The reason we go to poetry is not for wisdom, but for the dismantling of wisdom.' In this sense Rego dismantles the patriarchal story that has flattened girls and women everywhere, erasing their own desires to better serve those of everyone else, and replaces it with raw feeling. This is another kind of wisdom, always subversive, as in *Nursing* (2000), in which we gaze at the ambivalent feelings of a young woman nursing an elderly woman who lies prostrate on the armchair. The protagonist doing the caring has a flower in her hair. Life! Sexuality! She is resilient, enduring, her arms crossed, but what is transmitted is that she is both nursing and desiring at the same time. This is not easy to do, yet Rego's sheer technical virtuosity manages, always, to convey the poetry and complexity of mixed feelings.

The Fisherman (2005) pulls us into the surreal world of a doll-like child and a giant octopus with its tactile white belly and orange blistered tentacles. It seems to float in the deep of an inky black carpet that is also the ocean. A benign monster, the fisherman, sits next to a reclining woman on a mattress, his rod outstretched in what is both interior space and a landscape of rocks, weeds and parched riverbeds. If Rego mythically brings to the surface some of what lurks in the depths, it is usually to do with perplexing human relations.

This benign monster appears again in *Reading the Divine Tragedy by Dante* (2005), in which the female protagonist wears a sleeveless green dress, her bare muscular right arm folded across her lap. Yet the fingers of her left hand seem both shocked and contemplative as they rest on the tweed jacket, the arm of the smartly dressed monstrous creature reading her a book. His head is mostly a mouth. Near her feet a cicada seems to be listening too. And there she is again, or someone like her, floating in the right-hand corner, sipping wine with the Dante-reading creature. Meanwhile, another woman is mopping the floor while a cherub reaches out to touch the mop. Outside the window is the beach, turquoise sea and yellow sand, where women attend to their children. This morphing of realism and surrealism gives equal status to the ordinary and the extraordinary, in which, as ever, the artist is also working with fragments of memory. Apparently, her father would read Dante to her when she was a child.

Rego has suggested she doesn't like drawing self-portraits. For this reason, she has used her long-time model, Lila Nunes, as her alter ego. This in itself is a relationship to be noted for art history, a flip of the traditional male artist's muse. To transmit oneself through someone else, and for this uncanny metamorphosis to transparently be the game, adds a unique, perhaps even a metafictional dimension to much of the work. However, when Rego had a fall and bruised her face, it became more interesting to her to draw it.

The Self-Portrait series (2017) is a rare and significant part of Rego's archive, not least for its visceral sense of the artist staring piercingly at herself. We see an older woman, her mouth wide open to reveal a snarl of crooked lower teeth, a wedding ring (perhaps) on the finger of her left hand, a pastel stick held in her right hand. If she is stripped of the radiance of youth, she is nevertheless radiant with the force of her own taboo-breaking gaze. These valuable self-portraits have an affinity with Francis Bacon's 1950s Screaming Pope series, about which Bacon commented: 'I like, you may say, the glitter and colour that comes from the mouth, and I've always hoped in a sense to be able to paint the mouth like Monet painted a sunset.' The mouth in Rego's self-portraits is a whole landscape in itself, an abundance of life rendered in a few delicate lines. There is a sense of almost demonic possession in the one open eye that stares at herself. Perhaps it is the force of her desire to create art.

To encounter the 2007 series titled Depression is to understand that the full spectrum of female emotional life has been embodied for us by a uniquely fearless artist. This again is a note for art history, and not a footnote either. It is as if Rego acknowledges, yes, there is enchantment, desire, betrayal, fame, joy, imaginative flight, powerful sexuality, political purpose – most amplified in the Abortion series, *Untitled* (1999) – yes, there is magical thinking and love, yet there is this too.

Julia Kristeva evokes the heavy weight of depression in her sublime book on this subject, *Black Sun: Depression and Melancholia* (1992). Kristeva writes:

> Where does this black sun come from? Out of what eerie galaxy do its invisible, lethargic rays reach me, pinning me down to the ground, to my bed, compelling me to silence, to renunciation?

This resonates with Rego's reclining women in her Depression series, in that they seem pinned down by those invisible rays, thinking and breathing in a number of positions on a blazing yellow sofa. In the first drawing of this extraordinary series, a seated woman is encircled by the elaborate black frills and pleats of her almost Gothic dress. Its composition resembles the black sun of Kristeva's title, except the woman is not so much listless, as alert. The folds of this all-consuming costume seem to personify her malaise; the dress does all the talking for her. These long-skirted women are somehow ageless, universal. They could be the Brontë sisters, or Elizabeth Barrett Browning, or Virginia Woolf, or ourselves, or our mothers, yet in Rego's hands, as with all her girls and women, they are neither pathologized or shamed. This is the enduring legacy of one of the most skilled figurative artists in the world.

THE PSYCHOPATHOLOGY OF
A WRITING LIFE

Fiction is a good home for the reach of the human mind.
It can give shelter to all the dimensions of consciousness, including the unconscious. If the writer is hospitable
to this idea, and if the task interests us enough, we will find
our own literary strategies to build our home. Consciousness
in this regard does not mean streams of consciousness, but
rather the consciousness of the entire composition of our
story. This composition will have its own very particular writing behaviour, as Roland Barthes so beautifully told us.

And is it true that when we write we are only as interesting
as how we think and where we are looking or how we are
looking or what it is we are feeling and how that feeling is
connected to history (the personal and political past), or how

we are breathing when we explain why we slammed a door? The human mind can go anywhere. This is a good thing in art. In life this is not always a good thing. We know that unwelcome thoughts can torment us and that we ingeniously find our own private magic to see them off.

In art there is a place for this kind of private magic.

I'm guessing we become boring when our minds are numb and closed and when we cannot tolerate doubt, or when we have no interest in the subjectivities of others, or when, for many understandable reasons, we cannot access the (apparently) unknowing parts of our minds. When we create characters or avatars to carry our ideas into the worlds of our fictions, it is desirable to want to access the unknowing parts of their minds, as well as their more conscious motivations.

There is plenty of pressure to numb our minds. Corporate culture likes to reduce human experience to the many questionnaires we are invited to tick or cross. The questionnaire has implicitly written the story for us. We do not have to stutter and stumble and struggle for language or put to work the imaginative reach of our minds or put to work the skills a writer needs to hold many contradictory thoughts at the same time. With this in mind, it is important and exciting to say and think things we do not yet understand. If we are reaching for something that is there anyway, in ourselves, in the world, the struggle in the writing is to connect our thoughts and make visible something that is seemingly impossible to convey. When we pay too much attention to the commercial

health and safety regulations for getting published, it is likely
that our writing will become so hyper-intelligible that it tragically dies before it opens its eyes.

If coherence is achieved at the expense of complexity, it is not
really coherence. Perhaps it is just an opinion. Complexity
and coherence are twins, always in secret conversation with
each other. Any kind of coherence that flattens or sanitizes
the world of our fictions or offers false consolations for the
anxieties that make us interesting or resolves conflicts and
restores moral order in unbelievable ways, or that dulls the
awkward, fragile, illogical, incoherent parts of living a life,
simply does not have enough dimensions. The point of life is
to tune in to all its dimensions, including the ecology of the
natural world.

I started writing in the late twentieth century. My first novel
was published in 1987, two years before the Berlin Wall came
down and communist Eastern Europe started to unravel. I
wrote my first story on a typewriter, there was no Internet
and I made use of public libraries. Now I write on a MacBook
Pro and a MacBook Air and a desktop Mac. I use the Pro to
watch films, the Air to travel and write, and the desktop is in
my writing shed, usually with my mobile phone on the desk.

For my novel *Hot Milk*, I made use of handwritten journals
written in Almería, where the novel is set. I find that kind of
writing useful because it's a way of catching first thoughts

before they are censored and finessed. I also used Google to research the following subjects: how a sandblaster works, the physiology of a sigh, immigrant tomato pickers in southern Spain, how a handkerchief is arranged in the jacket pocket of an old-fashioned gentleman's suit. Facts. I really need them to tune the reality levels of my book so that I can do a deal with you, the reader, when I subvert the reality levels of my book. I can't subvert a reality unless I create a reality. I am constantly transferring material from the Air to the Pro and back to headquarters in the dark, dusty shed. So quite literally the writing itself is migrating across various technologies.

All the same, staring at the screen is not the same action as staring at the world. There is some contemporary confusion about this, and I argue my case in *Hot Milk*, through the character (or avatar for my arguments) of 25-year-old Sofia. She often gets lost staring at her screen and reckons she needs to risk coming down to earth where all the hard stuff happens. For a start, the screen does not stare back or love us or punch us in the face. It is not addicted to us, though we might be addicted to it. How we gaze at the world and how we negotiate the way it gazes back at us is at the core of all writing.

There is the story and then there is everything else. If we are not interested in everything else, we are probably not interested in language. You will have your own ideas about what everything else might be. All narrative is a Trojan Horse.

What is hiding in its belly and what is hiding in its mouth? It's always a very good thing to put a few drawing pins under the self-righteous bullying butt of narrative – we have got to keep it alert and make it scream a little and make sure it does not settle into an armchair with a kitten on its lap. Narrative loves itself too much and wants you to adore it too. Sometimes narrative is so begging, it actually passes around the chocolates and chuckles as it warms its hands by a crackling fire. As Rilke told us, it's never too late to attempt to truthfully and humbly describe a sorrow that can also make us laugh. It's always a pleasure when words and sentences land with the cadence in the right place, or when the reveal and conceal of the story is in the right place, or when the balance between enigma and coherence is in the right place.

I know that things are going well when there is something about a character that I cannot fully comprehend. The more unknowable they seem, the more fascinating they become to me. Perhaps this is just a trick to keep me writing. Sometimes I strike on something I did not know. I hear the sound of that strike, it sparks, I can smell the smoke. That kind of strike changes everything.

If I am an avant-garde writer and want my work to be appreciated for the beauty of its formal innovation, it would be an innovation to accelerate high emotion rather than avoid it completely for fear it will stain my shirt. If you are a sentimental writer, it would be an innovation to read some difficult theory and have no character feel anything at all until you figure out what is really being felt.

It is a writing adventure to go in deep, then deeper, and then to play with surface so that we become experts at surface and depth. It is possible to have a preference for the shallows or a preference for the depths, but I reckon they coexist anyway. In life, no one I know is entirely stupid or entirely clever. What do you think? If you don't enjoy thinking, I can't see how you will enjoy writing.

It's exciting to lose as much fear as possible when it comes to writing, because that's the only way to be open enough to make something new. There's never any point in straining to make something new, but usually when we do, it's because we have taken a risk. You will have your own ideas about what taking a risk means to you. So long as we do not pluck out the heart of our mystery (to misquote Shakespeare), there will always be something interesting to do with language.

TOO MUCH PAST

When the pandemic roared into the end of the second decade of our twenty-first century, the past become livelier in my mind. With the present and the future in flux, it was as if I had nowhere else to go. During the long days and nights of various lockdowns, I wondered if the past rudely visited me, ghostly, uninvited, or if I walked backwards, un-invited, to haunt it?

The main soundtrack in my life at this time was the wailing si-rens of ambulances taking Covid patients to hospital. Maybe it was because death was in the air that I found myself revisiting Chekhov's great play *The Three Sisters*, first performed in 1901 at the Moscow Art Theatre. When I was a theatre student, aged nineteen, a famous female director came to our college to create a production of this play – I was cast as melancholy, rebellious Masha. I think the director thought my high cheek-bones suited the role, but, alas, I had little acting talent. With hindsight (not my favourite sort of sight), maybe the director did not have much directing talent either.

These spirited sisters, Olga, Masha and Irina, all of them in their twenties, live on the edge of a small provincial Russian town. Their most fierce desire, it seems, after the death of their parents, is to return to cosmopolitan, cultured Moscow, which is where they were born. They love the past more than they love the present, and wish to return to it.

On the night of the performance, I sat on the stage chaise-longue in full costume, staring blankly into space, while Olga, my stage sister, spoke the first line in the play: 'It's exactly a year ago today that Father died, the fifth of May.' That this play begins on the anniversary of Masha, Olga and Irina's father's death did not mean very much to me at the age of nineteen. In fact, it seems to me now, aged sixty, that all of us young actors were trying to create an emotional mood we did not yet understand.

Why, I asked myself, as another ambulance rattled down the road, did the director not say to that cast of young people: 'May I ask if any of you have experienced the death of a parent?' And if just one of us had replied, 'Yes, my mother died when I was twelve,' the director would have been wise to ask if that student might share some of the thoughts and feelings that come out to play on the anniversary of a parent's death.

That way, I would not have been staring blankly into space on the first night of the performance.

And something else. Masha quotes from Pushkin at the start of the play: 'A green oak by the curving shore, and on that oak a chain of gold.' I sort of understood those lines, aged nineteen, but I did not feel them. Later, maybe thirty years later, when my marriage was on the rocks (as was Masha's in *Three Sisters*), I read Sylvia Plath's poem 'The Couriers': 'A ring of gold with the sun in it? Lies. Lies and a grief.' Oh, I thought, so *that's* what Masha was trying to convey.

As the Danish philosopher Søren Kierkegaard told us, 'Life can only be understood backwards; but it must be lived forwards.'

That ring of gold came back again, in a different form, when I joined a queue outside a London grocery store, all of us wearing surgical masks as if they were the most normal accessory in the world. Someone in the queue asked me if I had the time. It's a perfectly reasonable question, but the pandemic had somehow managed to congeal time, and anyway, these days everyone has the time on their phones. I found myself looking at my wrist, as if I had a watch strapped to it, which I did not. This gesture, glancing at a watch that was not there, brought back to me the memory of the little gold watch my paternal grandmother, who was born in Lithuania, bequeathed to me. I was seven when she died and it fitted my wrist perfectly.

Her name was Miriam Leah. When she arrived in Cape Town, aged twelve, in 1908, it was changed to Mary. Her future husband's name was Abraham Moses, and he had changed it to Mark. Mary and Mark. I still think of my grandmother as Miriam Leah, though I understand that Mary was her avatar to survive anti-Semitism. She was Mary like Mary Poppins, except she spoke English with a Yiddish accent. I'm not sure what happened to that watch, alas, but that afternoon, queueing to buy apricots, I realized that what I had inherited was not a 'grown-up' watch, as I had thought at seven, but a child's watch. It would not have fitted even the dainty wrists of Mary / Miriam when she was an adult woman.

Did Miriam Leah travel with that watch on the long journey from Lithuania to Cape Town? Why did I never ask her about that journey? Or, to put it another way, why was I not pointed by my family to ask her about the epic journey she had made with Rosa, her older sister? The train, the ship, the suitcases carried by a cart pulled by horses. Their mother had died of cancer and so the two sisters were obliged to join their es- tranged father in South Africa.

I would guess that Rosa and Miriam felt a bit tender on the anniversary of their mother's death. They would know how to speak the line 'It's exactly a year ago today that Mother died.' What happened to Miriam/Mary's relatives and the family friends who remained in Lithuania? Apparently, my grandmother told my father stories about the pogroms she had witnessed in her village, yet as an adult, he says, she never spoke of the holocaust. That silence was transmitted to me, too. I know nothing about my extended family in Lithuania. It is a silence I explore in my novel *Swimming Home*: 'If cities map the past with statues made from bronze forever frozen in one dignified position, as much as I make the past keep still and mind its manners, it moves and murmurs with me through every day.'

All the same, why is that gold watch important to me? What do I really want to know about it and what is it there to do?

This is one of the many questions that Maria Stepanova, Russian poet and writer of exquisite long-form prose, asks herself in her recent book, *In Memory of Memory*, a 500-page deep dive into historical, cultural and personal memory. In a sense she answers it in one punchy line: 'There comes a day when the scattered pieces of knowledge need to be fixed in a transmission line.'

Stepanova begins this discursive, epic meditation on and around the ways in which her 'ordinary' Jewish family managed to survive the persecutions of the twentieth century with the death of her father's estranged sister. The narrator finds herself in Aunt Galya's apartment, sorting through postcards, ivory brooches, photographs, letters, diaries, souvenirs. She realizes that this hoard is a valuable archive from the twentieth century.

'Objects from the long distant past,' Stepanova writes, 'look as if they have been caught in the headlights, they're awkward, embarrassingly naked. It's as if they have nothing left to do.'

Stepanova is at her most searing when she writes about the 'non-human face' of objects. Her description of missing parts of crockery as 'orphaned', or faded photographs as 'foundlings', opens the mind and lets in our own personal and historical associations. She is also astute on family photographs, noting there is always one which features 'a middle-aged, stylish woman, suffering from chronic, mild depression'.

Many writers are called upon by Stepanova to accompany her on what is as much a thought experiment 'on the way memory works, and what memory wants from me', as an attempt to piece together shattered fragments of family history. These include Sebald, Proust, Barthes, Nabokov, Sontag and, perhaps most piercingly, Osip Mandelstam, under the heading 'The Jewboy Hides from View'.

A few visual artists are enlisted too, but less successfully. Stepanova includes a short, rather basic treatise on the photography of Francesca Woodman, who experimented with ways of making herself blur and disappear in her self-portraits; also, the vibrant, turbulent, ironic paintings of Charlotte Salomon, who was murdered in Auschwitz. All the same, to twin these astonishing female artists who disappeared in different ways (Woodman suicided, aged twenty-two) is a brave idea. As Stepanova writes so evocatively in a chapter titled 'Selfies and Their Consequences', 'All that disappears is what made you yourself.' That is certainly true for the narrator in W. G. Sebald's 2001 novel, *Austerlitz*. He gradually manages to discover the fate of his mother, who was deported to the death camps. There is a great deal at stake for Jacques Austerlitz. This is because he carries within himself knowledge that is too painful to access. His assignment with the past is to recover this knowledge.

Stepanova's narrator speaks and thinks in a detached, elegant, serene tone. Perhaps there is no other tone that can better handle the panorama of ideas she puts to work in this philosophical investigation into remembering and forgetting. If I am not sure what is at stake or what her narrator wants to know, or indeed what it is she wishes to unknow, perhaps that's her point. 'There is too much past, and everyone knows it,' she tells us. As her title suggests, memory itself is an artefact.

> In contemporary Europe with its barely healed wounds, black holes, and traces of displacement, a well-preserved family archive is a rarity. A set of furniture and china that has come together over decades, inherited from aunts and grandmothers and once thought of as an ancient burden, now deserves its own special memorial. Those who were forced to flee (it hardly matters from whom they fled) burnt documents,

shredded photographs, cut off everything below the chin – officer epaulettes, army greatcoats, civil service uniforms – and left their papers with other people. By the end of the journey very little is left for the memory to cling to, and to set sail on.

It is sometimes a relief in this dense, intense, meandering stretch of writing, to come across an anchoring line, such as: 'My grandfather was from the southern port city of Odessa.' And a pleasure to learn that the cab drivers in Odessa 'sang opera arias as if they were gondoliers'. At the same time, the narrator tells us, 'News of pogroms spread like wildfire around Southern Ukraine. It travelled on trains with the railway men, down the Dniepr with the ferrymen, jostled at hiring fairs, and served as a model for new outbursts of pointless cruelty: "Let's do it the Kievan way!"'

Towards the end of the massive achievement that is *In Memory of Memory*, Stepanova writes, 'Sometimes it seems like it is only possible to love the past if you know it is definitely never going to return.' I know what she means. Chekhov understood this, too. The Three Sisters do not return to Moscow. Miriam Leah did not return to Lithuania. Yet, as Freud told us, the past does return, and though we might wish to see it off, the repressed will jump into the queue at the grocery store and present itself in the form of a child's gold watch. Memory was Freud's major subject, of course, a life's work. His archaeological metaphor suggests that to recover the past, with all its shards and fragments, we have to dig down and bring to the surface those memories that have been pushed out of consciousness. And so, for this reader anyway, the unconscious of *In Memory of Memory* is the way it obsessively digs up the perilous twentieth century and searches amongst its tram routes, crockery and stockings for the trauma wound.

The past is not exactly a stranger at our table, but it is uncanny all the same. Neither dead nor alive, it does not return my stare or smile or tears, but in my own mind it does listen to my thoughts. Somehow, I believe we are both of us, the present and past, slightly altered from this exchange of knowledge and feeling.

BLUE RAIN

People do not die for us immediately, but remain
bathed in a sort of aura of life which bears no relation
to true immortality but through which they continue
to occupy our thoughts in the same way as when they
were alive. It is as though they were travelling abroad.

—MARCEL PROUST,
IN SEARCH OF LOST TIME (1913–27)

Dear Peter,
     I bought a wisteria plant today (about two feet tall in
its pot) and carried it in the April weather (sunshine and snow)
to the tiny balcony of my apartment. Then I read the instructions, which told me that *Wisteria sinensis* is sometimes called
Blue Rain. That made me think of you because you were crazy
for *Purple Rain* and Prince died on this day, 21 April. So, Peter,
here I am in London thinking of you and Prince today, while
I settle in the wisteria.

     I wish so very much that I had seen you before you died
in Frankfurt. Amongst many other subjects (politics, art, sex,
new beers from Belgium, power, lack of power, madness –

you were reading Michel Foucault – the horror of Scotch eggs, money and how we did not have enough of it, the way people smile and if they mean it), we often discussed our respective mothers – which, we decided, was a conversation without end. All of the world is in Mother, every emotion, too. Love, rage, regret, fear, guilt, pity, admiration, the need to fly from her nest, her breast, her vintage problems (mine born in 1939), the sorrow in her eyes, the viper in her heart, the pains in her legs, oh God, didn't we have enough problems of our own? Do you remember how we continued this conversation in the rowing boat on the lake in Regent's Park?

I was in charge of the oars on that day, pulling our boat across the brackish water, steering it to change direction so we could sit under the trailing branches of a willow tree and begin our picnic of radishes and potato salad. Years later, after we lost touch with each other, I wrote a novel about a mother and daughter, titled *Hot Milk*. It's about how love can scald us, and how sometimes we are the arsonists. You never got to read it, or to discuss the low flame that burns underneath it, yet in a way I began to write it that afternoon with you in the rowing boat.

Meanwhile, back here in London, according to the instructions that come with the wisteria plant, I have to feed it with 'fish, blood and bone' to help it bud and make blue rain. Peter, I can see you gazing at me now. Your blue eyes are the rain. Did you and I mean the things we said all those years ago? I think we did.

We thought deeply and freely together, no shaming, no judgement, no righteous pointing fingers, so many hopeful words thrown at the wind. This is to say hello, again, my old friend.

Some of this writing was previously published in the following journals and assorted media:

'Bathed in an Arc of French Light': *Cent Magazine* (2004).

'Marguerite Duras': 'Book of a Lifetime: *The Lover* by Marguerite Duras', *Independent*, 29 September 2011.

'My Beautiful Brothel Creepers': 'Real Living: Love and Brothel Creepers', *Independent on Sunday*, 8 November 1998; *A Second Skin: Women Write About Clothes*, ed. Kirsty Dunseath (The Women's Press, 2000).

'Walking Out of the Frame': 'Francesca Woodman: Vanishing Act', *Tate Etc.*, 43 (Summer 2018).

'Believe It': 'My Hero: Lee Miller', *Guardian*, 21 September 2012.

'Kingdom Come': introduction to *Kingdom Come* by J. G. Ballard (Fourth Estate, 2014).

'Telegram to a Pylon Transmitting Electricity over Distances': *Artesian Journal*, ed. Gareth Evans (2008).

'A Mouthful of Grey': 'Touring London' (2000), InIVA.org.

'Them and Us': foreword to *Hysteria*, a graphic novel written by Richard Appignanesi, drawings by Oscar Zarate (Self-MadeHero, 2015).

'Ann Quin': *Music & Literature*, no. 7 (2016).

'A to Z of the Death Drive': commissioned by Jules Wright for Wapping Hydraulic Power Station for an exhibition by Dean Rogers, 2009; published in *Five Dials*, 30 (August 2015).

'Migrations to Elsewhere and Other Pains': *New Statesman* (April 2013).

'A Roaming Alphabet for the Inner Voice': *Revolver* (2006).

'Reading Violette Leduc's Autobiography, *La Bâtarde*': introduction to *La Bâtarde* by Violette Leduc (Dalkey Archive Press, 2009).

'The Lady and the Little Fox Fur': introduction to *The Lady and the Little Fox Fur* by Violette Leduc (Penguin, 2018); extracted in the *Guardian*, 25 August 2018.

'Charisma': written for Forced Entertainment's lecture performance *Marathon Lexicon* (2006).

'Mona Lisa': written for *1001 Nights*, a durational performance by Barbara Campbell (2008).

'The Position of Spoons': 'The Position of Teaspoons', *The Happy Reader* (June 2018).

'The Mortality Project 2050': *Southword 35*, ed. Patrick Cotter (2018).

'Watery Things': Whitstable Biennale 2018.

'Letter to a Stranger': *Dear Stranger: Letters on the Subject of Happiness* (Penguin, 2015).

'X = Freedom': a poem for Meret Oppenheim, commissioned and performed at the Swiss Institute, Rome, 2023.

'Seduction and Betrayal': introduction to *Seduction and Betrayal* by Elizabeth Hardwick (Faber & Faber, 2019).

'Lemons at My Table': *The Food Almanac* by Miranda York (Pavilion Books, 2020).

'Hope Mirrlees': foreword to *Paris: A Poem* by Hope Mirlees (Faber & Faber, 2020).

'*The Inseparables* by Simone de Beauvoir': introduction to the translation by Lauren Elkin (Vintage Classics, 2021).

'Paula Rego': extract from the essay 'She Doesn't Want It', *Paula Rego: The Forgotten* (Victoria Miro, 2021).

'The Psychopathology of a Writing Life': commissioned by Word Factory, 2016.

'Too Much Past': *Jewish Quarterly* (August 2021).

Deborah Levy writes fiction, plays, and poetry. Her work has been staged by the Royal Shakespeare Company, broadcast on the BBC, and translated widely. She is the author of several highly praised novels, including *August Blue*, *The Man Who Saw Everything* (long-listed for the Booker Prize), *Hot Milk* and *Swimming Home* (both Man Booker Prize finalists), *The Unloved*, and *Billy and Girl*; the acclaimed story collection *Black Vodka*; and a three-part autobiography, *Things I Don't Want to Know*, *The Cost of Living*, and *Real Estate*. She lives in London and is a fellow of the Royal Society of Literature.